# The Cost of Land Use ]

*Applying transaction cost economics to planning & development*

---

**Edwin Buitelaar**

Institute for Management Research
Department of Spatial Planning
Radboud University Nijmegen
The Netherlands

**Blackwell**
Publishing

Blackwell Publishing editorial offices:
Blackwell Publishing Ltd, 9600 Garsington Road, Oxford OX4 2DQ, UK
    Tel: +44 (0)1865 776868
Blackwell Publishing Inc., 350 Main Street, Malden, MA 02148-5020, USA
    Tel: +1 781 388 8250
Blackwell Publishing Asia Pty Ltd, 550 Swanston Street, Carlton, Victoria 3053, Australia
    Tel: +61 (0)3 8359 1011

First published 2007 by Blackwell Publishing Ltd

ISBN: 9781405151238

Library of Congress Cataloging-in-Publication Data

Buitelaar, Edwin.
    The cost of land use decisions : applying transaction cost economics to planning
    & development / Edwin Buitelaar. – 1st ed.
        p. cm.
    Includes bibliographical references and index.
    ISBN-13: 978-1-4051-5123-8 (pbk. : alk. paper)
    ISBN-10: 1-4051-5123-4 (pbk. : alk. paper)    1. Land use--Economic aspects.
    2. Land use—Case studies. 3. Land use--Planning. 4. Real estate development. I. Title.
    HD156.B85 2007
    333.73'15—dc22

                                                2006102876

A catalogue record for this title is available from the British Library
Set in 10/13 Trump Mediaeval
by Newgen Imaging Systems Pvt Ltd, Chennai
Printed and bound in Singapore
by COS Printers Pte Ltd

The publisher's policy is to use permanent paper from mills that operate a sustainable
forestry policy, and which has been manufactured from pulp processed using acid-free
and elementary chlorine-free practices. Furthermore, the publisher ensures that the text
paper and cover board used have met acceptable environmental accreditation standards.

For further information on Blackwell Publishing, visit our website:
www.blackwellpublishing.com

The Royal Institution of Chartered Surveyors is the mark of property professionalism worldwide, promoting best practice, regulation and consumer protection for business and the community. It is the home of property related knowledge and is an impartial advisor to governments and global organisations. It is committed to the promotion of research in support of the efficient and effective operation of land and property markets worldwide.

# Real Estate Issues

### Series Managing Editors

*Stephen Brown*   RICS
*John Henneberry*   Department of Town & Regional Planning, University of Sheffield
*David Ho*   School of Design & Environment, National University of Singapore
*Elaine Worzala*   Professor, Director of the Accelerated MSRE, Edward St. John Department of Real Estate, Johns Hopkins University.

*Real Estate Issues* is an international book series presenting the latest thinking into how real estate markets operate. The books have a strong theoretical basis – providing the underpinning for the development of new ideas.

The books are inclusive in nature, drawing both upon established techniques for real estate market analysis and on those from other academic disciplines as appropriate. The series embraces a comparative approach, allowing theory and practice to be put forward and tested for their applicability and relevance to the understanding of new situations. It does not seek to impose solutions, but rather provides a more effective means by which solutions can be found. It will not make any presumptions as to the importance of real estate markets but will uncover and present, through the clarity of the thinking, the real significance of the operation of real estate markets.

## Books in the series

Greenfields, Brownfields & Housing
Development
Adams & Watkins
978 0 632 06387 1

Planning, Public Policy & Property
Markets
Edited by Adams, Watkins & White
978 1 4051 2430 0

Housing & Welfare in Southern Europe
Allen, Barlow, Léal, Maloutas & Padovani
978 1 4051 0307 7

Markets and Institutions in Real Estate
& Construction
Ball
978 1 4051 1099 0

Housing, Neighbourhood Renewal &
Community Engagement
Edited by Beider
978 1 4051 3410 1

Urban Regeneration in Europe
Couch, Fraser & Percy
978 0 632 05841 2

Economics & Land Use Planning
Evans
978 1 4051 1861 3

Economics, Real Estate & the Supply
of Land
Evans
978 1 4051 1862 0

Development & Developers
Guy & Henneberry
978 0 632 05842 6

The Right to Buy
Jones & Murie
978 1 4051 3197 1

Economics of the Mortgage Market
Leece
978 1 4051 1461 5

Housing Economics & Public Policy
O'Sullivan & Gibb
978 0 632 06461 8

International Real Estate
Seabrooke, Kent & How
978 1 4051 0308 4

British Housebuilders
Wellings
978 1 4051 4918 1

The Cost of Land Use Decisions
Buitelaar
978 1 4051 5123 8

## Forthcoming

Building Cycles & Urban Development
Barras
978 1 4051 3001 1

Mortgage Markets Worldwide
Ben-Shahar, Leung & Ong
978 1 4051 3210 7

Urban Sprawl
Couch, Leontidou & Petschel-Held
978 1 4051 5123 8

Real Estate & the New Economy
Dixon, McAllister, Marston & Snow
978 1 4051 1778 4

Towers of Captial
Lizieri
978 1 4051 5672 1

Affordable Housing & the Property Market
Monk & Whitehead
978 1 4051 4714 9

Property Investment & Finance
Newell & Sieracki
978 1 4051 5128 3

Housing Stock Transfer
Taylor & Webb
978 1 4051 7032 1

Real Estate Finance in the New
Economic World
Tiwari & White
978 1 4051 5871 8

Housing Markets & Planning Policy
Jones & Watkins
978 1 4051 7520 3

Transforming the Private Landlord
Crook & Kemp

# Contents

# Preface

Doing a research project like the one that is presented in this book is often characterised by depths and heights. For me personally, from the very beginning, I have not experienced these strong fluctuations at all. Before joining the university in March 2002, I expected my academic career to be temporary and short. But I am afraid that this kind of work has grabbed me in a big way. The freedom that I have experienced, especially in the beginning, is something that can hardly be paralleled in any other working environment. This freedom needs to be accompanied by discipline and the will to explore on behalf of the researcher. But probably more importantly, it also needs to be matched by an academic environment that stimulates the exploration. This environment is made by people.

There is one person in particular that I want to thank for all his help during the process. Barrie Needham has proved to be a great teacher, source of inspiration, colleague and person. His honest curiosity for both theory and practice, his engagement with my project, and his constructive and stimulating attitude has made this research project a pleasant journey.

I also want to thank my colleagues in the department of Human Geography, Spatial Planning, and Political Sciences of the Environment. There are some who I would like to thank in particular, which are my colleagues from our thematic research group 'Land policy and location development': Esther Geuting, Peter Hendrixen, Wouter Jacobs, George de Kam, Erwin van der Krabben, Barrie Needham and Arno Segeren. This group is part of a larger team called Governance and Places (GaP), which is led both practically and substantively, in a very inspirational way, by Arnoud Lagendijk, who deserves to be thanked for creating such an environment. He has contributed to this book more than he is probably aware of. He and Esther Geuting are also gratefully acknowledged for reading, and making comments to, the manuscript as a whole.

This book includes comparative research, for which the willingness of many respondents and other people was needed. All these people – most of them mentioned and acknowledged in the Appendix – are thanked for sharing their knowledge and experiences. There is one person in particular that I want to thank in this respect, and that is Janet Askew from the University of the West of England. Her help has made

Chapter 5 much better than it would have been without, and made my stays in Bristol extremely interesting and entertaining.

Other people who had an important role at some stage in the research by making comments to a chapter or a paper, by pointing me to the right sources, or helping me in any other way are Ernest Alexander, Raffael Argiolu, Margo van den Brink, Dan Bromley, Andreas Faludi, Cecilia Giusti, Henri Goverde, Patsy Healey, Rob van der Heijden, Leonie Janssen-Jansen, Ton Kreukels, Michael Neuman, John Raggers and Roelof Verhage. Obviously, a good personal environment is the most important prerequisite for performing professionally. The people who are responsible for that are my parents, my brother and my friends. Thank you all!

# 1

# The Cost of Making Land Use Decisions

## Introduction

The song that would become the Beatles' last number one hit in the US, (in 1970), *The Long and Winding Road*, was most certainly not written by Paul McCartney with the evolution of our cities in mind. It is, however, applicable to them. In every country the built environment is continuously under construction: one land use is turned into another. This includes both the development of undeveloped greenfield land and the redevelopment of the existing urban fabric, the brownfield locations. However, these conversions do not occur instantly and without costs. Aside from the fact that a structure needs to be built, decisions have to be made about how the land should and should not be used. Because of this decision-making process, many projects take up much more time and cost than first intended. An interesting – though not uncommon – example is that of Hofpoort, a case study (Buitelaar *et al.*, 2006) in the city of Arnhem (in the Netherlands), where it took 10 years to deliver around 80 houses. A cynic could say that this project had a production of 8 houses a year. In many cases government regulation and the role of the government in general is held responsible for delays in the development process.

In the Netherlands, for instance, a task force responsible for investigating the reasons behind the lagging building production, concluded that the primary source was delays in the building process, caused mainly by the extensive permit system (Taskforce Woningbouwproductie, 2002).

Many developers also regard this as the main factor. It is said about planning in Britain that:

> 'The reality of land-use planning in Britain has often been one of institutional sclerosis and special-interest capture. Benefits have been concentrated on interest groups and bureaucrats with costs dispersed across an invisible mass of tax payers and consumers.'
>
> (Pennington, 2002, p. 71)

Recently, there have been many initiatives and intentions in many countries to cut rules and bureaucracy and to streamline procedures for land use planning. In France, for instance, a law (Loi SRU; urban solidarity and renewal law) was adopted in 2000, which intended, among other things, to break with the past desire to create detailed rules in the local land use plan. In England, the proposals to reform the planning system in the Planning Green Paper (from 2001) were mainly focused on reducing the complexity of the system and streamlining procedures. The Treasury was worried about economic competitiveness and, at the national level, a view prevailed that the planning system delayed development so much that England's competitiveness was suffering. However, at the same time, one of the (possibly contradictory) goals was to increase citizen participation during the development process. The Planning and Compulsory Purchase Act that was adopted in 2004 took over the main goals that were posed in the Planning Green Paper. In the Netherlands also, the cabinet is preparing a new planning act (that will probably be operational in 2008) that is driven partly by a desire to cut rules and to speed up the planning process. The maximum duration of the procedure for adopting a land use plan (the *bestemmingsplan*), which is the core planning document on the basis of which building permissions are granted or rejected, is halved in the new act. It remains to be seen in each of the above examples whether the goals of cutting rules, reducing complexity and streamlining procedures will really work out as intended. Looking at the first experiences in England, this seems most questionable.

More privatisation, more market, less bureaucracy and fewer rules are phrases that can be heard on a regular basis in almost every democratic country. In the US and the UK, this discourse took off significantly in the late 1970s and early 1980s when both Reagan and Thatcher came to power. In continental Europe it generally emerged a few years later. In the Netherlands, for instance, generally regarded as a highly regulated country, the mission statement of the Dutch cabinet (Balkenende 2), after its inauguration in 2003, was 'participation, more work and fewer rules'. It was argued that there were too many rules in every policy sector. In essence, this cabinet's strategy was a continuation of a neo-liberal discourse that had emerged in the mid-eighties when prime-minister Lubbers came to power. Recently, China and former members of the Warsaw Pact have also started following this line. This observed pressure on public intervention also applies to spatial planning or, as Sorensen (1994) puts it:

'Our era is reconsidering the ends and means of governments in general in view of limited public finance; concerns over national economic efficiency; and a growing community preference for individual responsibility, self help, and small government. Planning is not immune to these trends.' (Sorensen, 1994, p. 198)

This book is about the formal rules that are made and used to steer land use decisions. These are primarily public rules, but they can also be privately made, as in the case of covenants. Whatever the origin of the rules, all of them are applied at a site-specific level, and this application is not without costs. The relationship between the way land use institutions are made and used at the site-level, and the costs associated with this, form the core of this book. One of the key debates that always seems to be behind discussions on regulation and deregulation, is that of 'the market versus government' debate.

## Beyond the 'market versus the government' debates

The starting point of this book is the recurring and fascinating 'market versus government' debate, an argument that is also ongoing in academic fora (see, for an extensive account on the starting point, Buitelaar, 2003). For over two decades in the UK and the US (with the coming of Thatcher and Reagan), and for more than a decade in many continental European countries, there has been renewed interest in the idea of more private involvement in traditional government activities. Some academics claim that the 'market' is more efficient in coordinating land use decision-making (Ellickson, 1973; Pennington, 1999). The counter-argument from welfare economics is to say that the 'market' often fails to operate efficiently; as a result, correction by government intervention is justified (Pigou, 1920). In economics, the discussion is often held around the concepts of market and public failures.

In neo-classical economics, it is assumed that in perfectly competing markets, demand and supply will become equal at an equilibrium that leads to an optimal allocation of resources. But, in practice, markets are rarely (and might never be) fully competitive. If the competitive equilibrium cannot be achieved, there will be a sub-optimal allocation of resources[1]. Pigou (1920), who can be seen as the founding father of welfare economics, addresses these situations as market failures, and these market failures are the justifications for government interventions. To welfare economists, the task of land use planning is to take care of the goods, which the market will not provide, under-supplies (Webster, 1998) (e.g. public transport in remote rural areas) or oversupplies (e.g. office buildings).

One of the implicit assumptions of this welfare economic approach is the idea that when the market fails and the government intervenes, the latter will do so perfectly and without costs. In addition, it assumes that the government acts always and only in the public interest. These assumptions have led to an important counter reaction, where it is argued that there are not only market failures, but also public or government failures (Levacic, 1991; Lai, 1997; Webster, 1998; Pennington, 1999), or non-market failures (Wolf, 1979). These authors challenge the welfare economists' implicit assumption of an imperfect market allocation versus a perfect administrative process of allocation. This assumption would suggest that planning is without costs, which it is obviously not, and also that a public body is always able to find and apply the best correction (see, for an extensive enumeration of planning costs, Sorensen, 1994, p. 198).

So, although markets often do not succeed in achieving economically efficient results, government intervention is not necessarily a guarantee for achieving these either (Levacic, 1991, p. 45). Welfare economics and the idea of a costless, selfless and perfectly operating government, *in casu* a planning agency, have their shortcomings[2], and one

---

[1] By optimal allocation, I mean 'economic' or 'allocative' efficiency. Allocation is more efficient if more goods and services are produced, or if goods and services are produced which people value more highly.

[2] This is often argued by public choice theorists, who start from the assumption made in many economic theories that rational actors are characterised by self-interested behaviour. In line with this, public choice theory argues that government serves itself rather than the public interest.

can conclude that both the market and the government have their failures (Wolf, 1988; CPB, 1999). However, this discussion over the failure of the market and the failure of the government does not take us any further. In welfare economics, every situation that is not optimal is qualified as inefficient or as a 'failure'. But as these optima are hardly ever reached, there is only failure, and this significantly devalues failure as a concept for judging the allocation of resources.

In addition, the reality is often too complex to fit within the neat dichotomy of 'the government' versus 'the market' (Dixit, 1996; Buitelaar, 2003) and 'planning' versus 'the market' (Lai, 1997; Alexander, 1992, 2001a,b). It is not helpful to regard the government and planning on one side and the market on the other as opposing forces (Alexander, 2004), since they are not mutually exclusive. The market is structured by the government that makes the rules that facilitate exchange. In addition, the government can be, and often is, a market actor. Comparing the market to the government, therefore, is like comparing apples and pears.

For these reasons, I start from a different perspective. Many land use decisions are made by many agents and agencies, and these have to be coordinated. 'Without co-ordination these agents and agencies might all have different and potentially conflicting objectives resulting in chaos and inefficiency' (Thompson *et al.*, 1991, p. 3)[3]. Coordination can be seen as '…the bringing together of otherwise disparate activities or events. Tasks and efforts can be made compatible by co-ordinating them' (Thompson *et al.*, 1991, p. 3). This coordination can be fulfilled in different ways. There are various *governance structures* (Williamson, 1975, 1985), or *models of coordination* (Thompson *et al.*, 1991), that can be distinguished, and these will be set out in more detail in Chapter 2.

Transaction cost economics[4] assumes that the choice of one structure above another depends – when all other variables are equal – on

---

[3] Some (e.g. Scharpf, 1993, p. 125) argue that the need for coordinating the choices of actors, is increasing through an increased interdependence and differentiation of interests.

[4] Although transaction cost economics is a more specialised strand than the broader new institutional economics (Williamson, 1993), both are used interchangeably. In my view, the difference is more in the label and the message it is supposed to send; the label 'transaction cost economics' is used to emphasise the importance of transaction costs, whereas new institutional economics illuminates the importance of institutions. Since this research focuses on both transaction costs and institutions, both labels will be used, depending on what I want to stress.

the nature of the transaction and the costs that result from it. This theory describes and prescribes which institutional design (more specifically, which governance structure) is currently and should in the future be aligned to which type of transaction. Transaction costs are the independent variables and the governance structures the dependent variables. This version of transaction cost theory has also been endorsed in planning theory (Alexander, 2001a). What these accounts somehow neglect to show, is that setting up and using institutions also involves costs, which I also classify under the heading transaction costs. The focus in this book is on the relationship between transaction costs and institutions, and especially the effect of institutions on transaction costs. There is very little empirical knowledge in land use planning and land economics covering this. In the development process, one land use is converted into another; but the same occurs for the institutional arrangements with regard to land use as these are also converted (Healey, 1992). How does this work? The goal of this book is to gain more insight into the nature of the institutions and related transaction costs in the production process of the built environment (i.e. the development process). What makes this particularly complicated is the multiple character of the concept 'institution'. Institutions occur at different levels and in different ways. In addition, institutions are dependent and independent variables at the same time. Gualini illustrates this nicely for planning, by saying that planning is at the same time 'an institutionalised practice' and 'a factor of institutionalisation' (Gualini, 2001, p. 55). This study tries to handle this multiplicity, its complexity and dynamics, by looking at the relationship between different institutional levels and how this in turn affects transaction costs. The central question that emerges from this is: how are the different institutional levels and transaction costs interrelated under different circumstances, and how does this affect the existence, size and incidence of transaction costs in the development process?

## The study of transaction costs in planning and property research

There is a field of study that can be called economics and planning. Economic analyses of planning have been carried out for some decades now, and many textbooks have appeared in the past (see e.g. Harrison,

1977; Evans, 1985), and recently a new wave of textbooks has emerged (Heikkila, 2000; Webster & Lai, 2003; Evans, 2004; Oxley, 2004; Needham, 2006b). Some of these (Heikkila 2000; Evans 2004) follow the mainstream economic tradition and analyse the (welfare) economic effects of planning (although Heikkila briefly pays attention to new institutional economics in the last chapter of his book). Others follow new pathways that are closer to this book. Webster & Lai (2003) combine insights from Hayekian economics, with public choice and new institutional economics, in order to explain how organisations, institutions and cities emerge and change. By applying ideas from Barzel (1998), a very close link and overlap with law and economics can be seen. The first comprehensive book about this branch of literature in combination with planning has been written by Needham (2006b). Although law and economics could be seen as a part of (or closely related to) new institutional economics, it differs in the way that it is a combination of two disciplines (not surprisingly: law and economics). It finds its roots in both disciplines, whereas new institutional economics, originates mainly from one discipline, as a group of economists were dissatisfied with the a-institutional nature of neo-classical and welfare economics. A more elaborate treatment of the differences between new institutional economics and law and economics can be found in Chapter 2. This book builds upon the aforementioned disciplines, by exploring 'new' theories from economics and applying them empirically.

With the focus set out above, this study lies not only on the interface between economics and planning, but also between planning and property research. This study could be regarded as being part of the institutional turn that has emerged in both fields. With respect to planning theory, Gualini (2001) speaks of an institutional turn, which follows the earlier identified argumentative turn (Fischer & Forester, 1993) or communicative turn (Healey, 1996; Innes, 1995). In property research, neo-classical and, to a lesser extent, Marxist approaches have for a long time dominated research on the development process. Due to a lack of appreciation for the interaction between structure and agency (see e.g. Ball, 1998; Healey, 1992), an institutional turn in property research emerged in the early nineties (see Guy & Henneberry, 2000). Although the number of contributions with an institutional perspective has risen (see e.g. Healey, 1992; Van der Krabben, 1995; Ball, 1998; Keogh & D'Arcy, 1999), it is still a very small stream compared to the vast majority of scholars that take a mainstream economic stance.

In planning theory, two streams within the institutional turn have been identified (Gonzalez & Healey, 2005): the sociological (e.g. Innes, 1995; Healey, 1997; Gualini, 2001) and the economic institutional (or transaction cost) strand (Alexander, 1992, 2001a; Lai, 1994, 1997; Webster & Lai, 2003; Webster, 1998; Buitelaar, 2004; for a comprehensive overview of contributions to transaction cost economics and planning see, Lai, 2005). Although they are set out as two separate and almost incompatible strands, both approaches are combined here. As the cases will show, transaction costs are not made by agents that act independently of others and solely pursue economic self-interest; in fact the actions of these agents are embedded in social structures (Granovetter, 1985). Transaction costs, in other words, are the result of continuous structure–agent relations. By making this amendment, transaction cost economics becomes a very useful analytical framework, which should not be rejected, (as some do), on the grounds of its objectivist ontology and oversimplified psychology of rationally acting individuals.

There is scepticism towards the integration of transaction cost economics and planning (Poulton, 1997; Moulaert, 2005), which I share when it comes to transaction cost theory as an explanatory theory for institutional change (Buitelaar *et al.*, 2006). The quest for reducing transaction costs as a determinant for institutional change, or even more broadly, as determinants of the emergence and evolution of cities (Webster & Lai, 2003), as often assumed, remains unproven and seems to be only part of the explanation of the emergence, continuity and change of socially constructed institutions. Nevertheless, transaction cost economics provides interesting analytical tools to investigate and compare institutional arrangements in theory and practice. In addition, 'the comparative institutional analysis of the world of positive transaction costs is a worthy challenge'. (Williamson, 1993)

Although the attention on transaction cost economics has increased, empirical applications of transaction cost theory in general, but in planning and property research in particular, are rare (see, for one of the very few examples, Needham & De Kam, 2004). This study seeks to identify transaction costs empirically and to understand their existence, size and distribution. It will not provide exact figures of transaction costs, nor calculate a total amount. This is almost impossible as transaction costs are often hidden, indirect and are not all quantified (in terms of money, man hours etc.) by the people involved in the development process. Where possible, an indication of the size of the transaction costs will be given.

## The relevance for planning practice

This study should be relevant to planning in two ways. The first is the 'market versus government' debate in planning, which has remained topical throughout the years. This has often been held in the same way, namely seeing the two forces as opposing one another (see e.g. Dahrendorf, 1966; Klosterman, 1985), and the economic approaches applied usually employ the same (neo-classical and welfare economic) language. I argue (see also, Buitelaar, 2003) that this is a fruitless and counterproductive discussion that should be approached differently. Approaching an old debate by a different language could shed a refreshing light that might serve planning theory well, and planning practice too, when thinking about institutional design. Transaction cost economics is a more pragmatic approach that can be used to compare realistic alternative institutional arrangements.

There is a second potential benefit that this book could have for planning and development practice. If we know how to identify transaction costs, and why they are made and distributed as they are, we might be able to reduce them, or redistribute them better. There are some transaction costs that contribute to better land use decisions, by whatever criterion (e.g. spatial quality or legitimacy) that is measured. What is also interesting is which transaction costs can be seen as dead-weight losses, in other words, a waste of money and time. Identifying particularly those dead-weight costs might help to improve the efficiency of planning practice and the development process. This could be done in policy and institutional evaluations.

## The structure of this book

In Chapter 2, I explore the literature on institutions and transaction costs, and illuminate the relationship between them. The main source of inspiration here is the institutional economic literature, but supplemented with insights from sociological institutionalism. This leads to a broad conceptual framework that indicates different institutional levels and how they impact on transaction costs. A distinction is made between macro-, meso- and micro-level institutions. In Chapter 3, both institutions and transaction costs are operationalised for the empirical research, focusing in particular on the micro-level institutions, since this is the level at which transaction costs are directly produced.

Applying land use law at the local level involves costs: transaction costs. However, a development process does not start and develop in an institutional void. There are rules of the game – the meso-level institutions – that set the stage within which the site-specific regime (i.e. the user rights regime as I call it in Chapter 3) is created and used. Therefore, Chapter 3 also pays attention to the meso level, which includes the formal land use institutions that can be used and applied at the site level. In addition the research strategy for the empirical part is set out in more detail.

Chapters 4, 5 and 6, deal with one case study each, showing which transaction costs are made during the development process of a small housing site as the result of the creation and use of the micro-level institutions. Each chapter starts with an exploration of the most important meso-level institutions in each country (like the planning act) that each stakeholder has to take into consideration. The three case studies are from Nijmegen (the Netherlands), Bristol (England) and Houston (Texas, United States). After analysis of each case study, they are compared to each other (Chapter 7). What follows from this chapter are some of the most discriminating dimensions with regard to transaction costs, which do not stand on their own but are related to deeper social and cultural norms and values (i.e. the macro institutions). Contextualising the transaction costs – which is done in Chapter 8 – provides an important part of the explanation of their existence, size and distribution. Chapter 9 contains the conclusions, in which the findings of the empirical section are confronted with the transaction cost theories of planning. In addition, some key issues in planning practice are fundamentally discussed from a transaction cost perspective.

# References

Alexander, E. R. (1992) A transaction cost theory of planning. *Journal of the American Planning Association* **58**(2): 190–200.

Alexander, E. R. (2001a) A transaction-cost theory of land use planning and development control. Toward the institutional analysis of public planning. *Town Planning Review* **72**: 45–75.

Alexander, E. R. (2001b) Why planning vs. markets is an oxymoron: asking the right question. *Planning and Markets* **4**(1).

Alexander, E. R. (2004) Capturing the public interest, promoting planning in conservative times. *Journal of Planning Education and Research* **22**: 102–6.

Ball, M. (1998) Institutions in British property research: a review. *Urban Studies* **35**(9): 1501–17.

Barzel, Y. (1998) *Economic Analysis of Property Rights.* Cambridge University Press, Cambridge.

Buitelaar, E. (2003) Neither market nor government. Comparing the performance of user rights regimes. *Town Planning Review* **74**(3): 315–30.

Buitelaar, E. (2004) A transaction-cost analysis of the land development process. *Urban Studies* **41**(13): 2539–53.

Buitelaar, E., Lagendijk, A. & Jacobs, W. (2007) A theory of institutional change: illustrated by Dutch city-provinces and Dutch land policy. *Environment and Planning A* **39**(4): 891–908.

Buitelaar, E., Mertens, H., Needham, B. & De Kam, G. (2006) *Sturend Vermogen en Woningbouw: Een Onderzoek naar het Vermogen van Gemeenten om te Sturen bij de Ontwikkeling van Woningbouwlocaties.* DGW/NETHUR, Den Haag/Utrecht.

CPB (1999) *De Grondmarkt: Een Gebrekkige Markt en een Onvolmaakte Overheid.* Sdu Uitgevers, Den Haag.

Dahrendorf, R. (1966) *Markt Und Plan: Zwei Typen Der Rationalität.* Mohr, Tuebingen.

Dixit, A. K. (1996) *The Making Of Economic Policy: A Transaction-Cost Politics Perspective.* MIT Press, Cambridge MA.

Ellickson, R. C. (1973) Alternatives to zoning: covenants, nuisance rules, and fines as land use controls. *The University of Chicago Law Review* **40**: 681–781.

Evans, A. (1985) *Urban Economics.* Basil Blackwell, Oxford.

Evans, A. (2004) *Economics & Land Use Planning.* Blackwell, Oxford.

Fischer, F. & Forester, J. (eds) (1993) *The Argumentative Turn in Policy Analysis and Planning.* Duke University Press, London.

Gonzalez, S. & Healey, P. (2005) A sociological institutionalist approach to the study of innovation in governance capacity. *Urban Studies,* **42**(11): 2055–69.

Granovetter, M. (1985) Economic action and social structure: the problem of embeddedness. *The American Journal of Sociology* **91**(3): 481–510.

Gualini, E. (2001) *Planning and the Intelligence of Institutions: Interactive Approaches to Territorial Policy-Making between Institutional Design and Institution Building.* Ashgate, Aldershot.

Guy, S. & Henneberry, J. (2000) Understanding urban development processes: integrating the economic and the social in property research. *Urban Studies* **37**(13): 2399–416.

Harrison, A. J. (1977) *Economics and Land Use Planning.* Croom Helm, London.

Healey, P. (1992) An institutional model of the development process. *Journal of Property Research* **9**: 33–44.

Healey, P. (1996) The communicative turn in planning theory: theory and its implications of spatial strategy formation. *Environment and Planning B: Planning and Design* **23**: 217–34.

Healey, P. (1997) *Collaborative Planning: Shaping Places in Fragmented Societies.* Macmillan, Basingstoke.

Heikkila, E. J. (2000) *The Economics of Planning*. Center for Urban Policy Research, New Brunswick NJ.

Innes, J. E. (1995) Planning theory's emerging paradigm: communicative action and interactive practice. *Journal of Planning Education and Research*, **14**(3): 183–9.

Keogh, G. & D'Arcy, É. (1999) Property market efficiency: an institutional economics perspective. *Urban Studies* **13**: 2401–14.

Klosterman, R. E. (1985) Arguments for and against planning. *Town Planning Review* **56**: 5–20.

Lai, L. W. C. (1994) The economics of land-use zoning. A literature review and analysis of the work of Coase. *Town Planning Review* **65**: 77–98.

Lai, L. W. C. (1997) Property rights justifications for planning and a theory of zoning. In: D. D. B. H. Massam (ed.), *Progress in Planning*, pp. 161–245. BPC Wheatons, Exeter.

Lai, L. W. C. (2005) Neo-institutional economics and planning theory. *Planning Theory* **4**(1): 7–19.

Levacic, R. (1991) Markets and government: an overview. In: J. F. G. Thompson, R. Levacic & J. Mitchell (eds), *Markets, Networks & Hierarchies: The Coordination of Social Life*, pp. 35–47. Sage, London.

Moulaert, F. (2005) Institutional economics and planning theory: a partnership between ostriches? *Planning Theory* **4**(1): 21–32.

Needham, B. (2006b) *Planning, Law And Economics: The Rules We Make For Using Land*. Routledge, London.

Needham, B. & De Kam, G. (2004) Understanding how land is transacted: markets, rules and networks, as illustrated by housing associations. *Urban Studies* **41**(10): 2061–76.

Oxley, M. (2004) *Economics, Planning And Housing*. Palgrave Macmillan, Basingstoke/New York.

Pennington, M. (1999) Free market environmentalism and the limits of land use planning. *Journal of Environmental Policy and Planning* **1**: 43–59.

Pennington, M. (2002) *Liberating the Land. The Case for Private Land-Use Planning*. The Institute of Economic Affairs, London.

Pigou, A. C. (1920) *The Economics of Welfare*. Macmillan, London.

Poulton, M. C. (1997) Externalities, transaction costs, public choice and the appeal of zoning. A response to Lai Wai Chung and Sorensen. *Town Planning Review* **68**: 81–92.

Scharpf, F. W. (1993) Coordination in hierarchies and networks. In: F. W. Scharpf (ed.), *Games in Hierarchies and Networks*, pp. 125–65. Westview Press, Boulder CO.

Sorensen, T. (1994) Further thoughts on Coasian approaches to zoning. A response to Lai Wai Chung. *Town Planning Review* **65**: 197–203.

Taskforce Woningbouwproductie (2002) *Achterblijvende Woningbouwproductie: Problematiek en Maatregelen*. VROM, Den Haag.

Thompson, G., Frances, J., Levacic, R. & Mitchell, J. (eds) (1991) *Markets, Hierarchies & Networks: The Coordination of Social Life*. Sage, London.

Van der Krabben, E. (1995) *Urban Dynamics: A Real Estate Perspective. An Institutional Analysis of the Production of the Built Environment* (dissertation). Thesis Publishers, Amsterdam.

Webster, C. J. (1998) Public choice, Pigouvian and Coasian planning theory. *Urban Studies* **35**: 53–75.

Webster, C. J. & Lai, L. W. C. (2003) *Property Rights, Planning and Markets: Managing Spontaneous Cities*. Edward Elgar, Cheltenham/Northampton MA.

Williamson, O. E. (1975) *Markets and Hierarchies*. Free Press, New York.

Williamson, O. E. (1985) *The Economic Institutions of Capitalism: Firms, Markets, Relational Contracting*. Free Press, New York.

Williamson, O. E. (1993) Transaction cost economics meets Posnerian law and economics. *Journal of Institutional and Theoretical Economics* **149**(1): 99–118.

Wolf, C. (1979) A theory of nonmarket failure: framework for implementation analysis. *The Journal of Law and Economics* **22**: 107–39.

Wolf, C. (1988) *Markets or Governments: Choosing between Imperfect Alternatives*. MIT Press, Cambridge MA.

# 2

# Institutions and Transaction Costs

---

This chapter contains an exploration and analysis of the role of institutions and transaction costs in economic theory, most notably within new institutional economics. First, a brief overview will be given of when and how institutions entered economics, together with a conceptual exposition of the kind of institutions that can be distinguished in various branches of economic research. After that, I will focus more specifically on the role and place of institutions and transaction costs within the new institutional economics, as it emerged from the work of Ronald Coase. Institutions will be confined to and divided into property rights and governance structures, two elements that play an important role in the production of the built environment at the micro-level. Transaction costs and how they emerge, according to transaction cost economists, will be discussed after that. This chapter concludes with a section in which transaction costs and institutions will be linked again, leading to a conceptual framework that serves to guide the analysis.

## Economic approaches to institutionalism

*The proper subject-matter of economic theory is institutions [...]*
(Hamilton, 1919)

Neo-classical economics probably originated in the classical economist Adam Smith's *Wealth of Nations* (1904) [1776], and focuses on markets, on how equilibriums are achieved and what the role of prices is. The market is usually seen as a self-adjusting system (the so-called 'invisible hand'), in which the price mechanism adjusts demand and supply in such a way that an equilibrium is reached in the end.

In the early twentieth century there was a reaction against this dominant neo-classical paradigm, from what we would now call 'old' or 'original' institutionalism[1] (e.g. Commons, 1931). In general, there are three sorts of criticism to neo-classical economics (Hazeu, 2000). The first is the level of abstraction of the theories, attributed to the inclination to be an exact science and not one that deals with human interactions. Second, neo-classical economics has been criticised for its limited empirical basis. The last, and arguably most important, flaw is in its image of the motives of human action. To facilitate mathematical formulation and exposition, neo-classical economists adopt psychologically unrealistic behavioural assumptions, such as viewing individuals and firms as rational maximisers (Posner, 1993). As a reaction against this, Veblen (1899) introduced the term 'conspicuous consumption', which he explained by arguing that rich people often do not prefer more expensive goods over the cheaper ones because they are better or nicer, but because their choice shows their prosperity. This does not correspond with the neo-classical behavioural assumption of rationally acting humans. The original institutionalists argue that people also have irrational preferences, and that actors do not act autonomously but are influenced by institutions and relations with others, which makes their preferences not only irrational but also relational (see e.g. Veblen and the importance of fashion). In line with this, notions such as the 'institutionalised individual' (Hodgson, 2000) or 'cultural animal' (Dequech, 2002) are used. Therefore, although the neo-classical approach focuses on markets, it is not very good at explaining how markets work (Hodgson, 2000), because it does not take account of institutions.

The old institutionalist branch in economics was not taken completely seriously by economists, to say the least, because it was not found very academic, and because it refuted the neo-classical paradigm almost entirely. Coase (1984, p. 230) said about it that: 'without a theory they had nothing to pass on except a mass of descriptive material waiting for a theory, or a fire.' However, (relatively) recently, it seems as if a new wave of old institutionalism has emerged (e.g. Hodgson, 1988; Dequech, 2002).

---

[1] What this strand is called differs. Many use the modifier 'old', while other use 'original', probably because it has a more positive connotation than 'old', which is close to old-fashioned. Yet others use no modifiers at all and talk about 'institutional economics'.

Like the old historical-descriptive institutionalists, the new institutionalists recognised that neo-classical economics was overly abstract (Furubotn & Richter, 1991). However, new institutional economics (which goes back to Coase, 1937) did not reject the micro-economic approach altogether, but gradually adjusted it, by adding the institutional component (Furubotn & Richter, 1991; Hazeu, 2000). What new institutional economics shares with old institutionalism is the attention to institutions. Where it differs from old institutionalism is in its treatment of neo-classical economic assumptions, as just mentioned, and also in its attention to the role and the type of institutions.

## Formal and informal institutions

A very common distinction made in the literature on institutions, is between formal and informal institutions (Bromley, 1989, p. 41; North, 1990, makes a similar distinction between conventions and rules). Formal institutions can be understood as institutions with a legal character, like legal norms and contracts. Informal institutions include conventions, habits and informal social norms, in other words, institutions that are not legally enforceable, but nevertheless influence our actions.

Within new institutional economics, though there are exceptions, the main emphasis is on formal institutions like contracts and property rights, and less on informal institutions such as habits and conventions, which the old institutionalists emphasise (Dequech, 2005). Some accuse new institutional economics of overemphasising the restrictive function of institutions on actions, and not taking account of the deeper cognitive function they have (Dequech, 2002)[2]. This critique is valid, since there is indeed very little attention paid to the manner in which institutions frame the way actors look upon the world. The reason is probably the focus on formal rules rather than informal practices. Nevertheless, formal rules too, like planning regulations, have their symbolic meaning. An example is zoning in the US, and in Houston in particular (see Chapter 6). In Houston, the debate about the introduction of zoning is very ideological since it has become

---

[2] In this sense, the old institutional economics is closer to sociological or political institutionalism. Pierre, a political institutionalist, defines institutions as '... overarching systems of values, traditions, norms, and practices that shape or constrain political behavior.' (Pierre, 1999, p. 373)

a clash between people who ask for government intervention to prevent negative externalities, versus people who want the market and private freedom to flourish (Buitelaar, forthcoming).

The restrictive function and deeper cognitive function are, however, to some extent interrelated. An instrumental (and restrictive) rationality is often socially highly appropriate, since people want problems to be solved (Buitelaar *et al.*, 2007). But the disregard of the deeper cognitive function and symbolic meaning of institutions is probably more a result of a focus on formal instead of informal institutions. This is because restrictions are often seen as something external to the actions of people, while informal institutions – for example habits – are often regarded as being internalised by the actors.

The primary attention on formal institutions brings new institutional economics close to law and economics, which both originate from the same source: Ronald Coase[3]. The Nobel Prize he won in 1991 was awarded primarily on the basis of his two classic papers: *The nature of the firm* (Coase 1937) and *The problem of social cost* (Coase 1960). His article from 1937 is a seminal paper for transaction cost economics, while his 1960 paper is one of the key sources of law and economics. Law and economics is literally concerned with economic analyses of law (see e.g. Cooter & Ulen, 2004). The core of the law and economics approach is similar to that of neo-classical micro-economics. Micro-economics – among other things – investigates and predicts how organisations and individuals react to prices and price differences. Law and economics, similarly, tries to predict how (economic) actors will behave with regard to law, for instance, the introduction or change of legal sanctions. There is considerable overlap between law and economics and transaction cost economics. One of the leading theorists in law and economics, Richard Posner, says they diverge on their theoretical emphasis. According to him, transaction cost economics is preoccupied with transaction costs, which leads it away from price theories and the mechanism of utility maximisation that are central to traditional neo-classical economics and law and economics (Posner, 1993, p. 83).

In this study the primary focus is on the formal institutions that stem from planning and property law, how they are used and how

---

[3] Posner (1993), however, argues that beside Coase there are three other founding fathers of law and economics. According to Williamson (1993), this does too little justice to Coase's prominence.

these affect transaction costs. But the informal institutions are not neglected as they have an important impact on the way the formal rules are used, and hence on the transaction costs.

## Institutions and transaction costs in the (early) new institutional economics

Although the origin of new institutional economics goes back to Ronald Coase's article *The nature of the firm* (1937), it was not until the early seventies, and especially until Williamson's *Markets and hierarchies* (1975), that new institutional economics received attention from 'mainstream' economics. Coase's work got attention retrospectively, according to himself, due to a hesitancy among economists to appreciate the role of markets, firms and laws in economic systems, as he illuminated in all his work (Coase, 1988).

In *The nature of the firm*, Coase asks the very basic question: if the price mechanism regulates production, as argued by many mainstream economists, then why do organisations (like firms) exist at all? Neoclassical economists assume that demand and supply, consumption and production, are adjusted to each other automatically, elastically and responsively. In the economic system there is no central control since it 'works itself'. However, Coase (1937) argues that this description of the economic system does not fit very well for transactions within a firm, which he describes as 'islands of conscious power', as distinct from the automatic and atomistic market system. If somebody in a firm moves from one department to another, he does not do that because of a change in price but because he is ordered to do so. This is what Coase calls 'economic planning'. Others (Bradach & Eccles, 1989) talk about 'authority' as the coordinating mechanism in these hierarchical forms of coordination.

Coase's central argument is that firms arise because there is a cost of using the price mechanism. There are, for instance, the costs of discovering what the price is. In addition, there are costs involved in negotiating and concluding every single contract. Later (e.g. Williamson, 1975), these costs were called transaction costs. Firms are set up, or expanded, to minimise those costs. Although firms, or organisations in general, have the ability to reduce transaction costs they cannot eliminate them. Moreover, they produce organisational costs. According to Coase, firms are expanded or downsized on the basis of the returns from the size of the hierarchy. When more hierarchy means increasing returns, a firm is likely to expand, while 'diminishing returns to management' (as Coase phrases it) leads to shrinking firms, which may, for instance, start hiving off activities to other firms. To explain the size of the firm and the way entrepreneurs decide about that, Coase uses the principle of *marginalism* (from Walras, 1874), which is central to neo-classical economics.

> 'Will it pay to bring an extra exchange transaction under the organizing authority? At the margin, the costs of organizing within the firm will be equal either to the costs of organizing in another firm or to the costs involved in leaving the transaction to be "organized" by the price mechanism.'                          (Coase, 1937, p. 405)

Coase (1988, p. 6) complains that *The nature of the firm* was much cited but little used. The reason, according to him, why transaction costs did not (until later) become part of the equipment of the economist, was that it did not fit in the conventional analyses that assumed the market to function without frictions. Others (Williamson, 1975) assert that the concept was not sufficiently operationalised to permit systematic analyses of transactions in relation to governance structures (like markets and firms)[4]. The main contribution of the *Nature of the firm* is that Coase draws our attention to *transaction costs*, as the discriminating factor for the mode of governance. In his 1960 paper – *The problem of social cost* – he builds on his earlier contribution, but his emphasis is slightly different; in that paper he shows us mainly the importance of *institutions* – in particular property rights – for economic exchange.

In *The problem of social cost*, Coase deals with the issue of the social costs of individual actions that was earlier addressed by the welfare economist Pigou (1920), in *The economics of welfare*. However, Coase approaches the issue differently. Pigou argues (see also Chapter 1) that in the case of market failures the government should intervene, for instance by levying taxes or imposing regulations. Such failures are often the negative social effects (externalities) caused by individual action. Both Pigou (1920) and Coase (1960) use the British example of

---

[4] However, Williamson values Coase's contributions highly. Together with Kenneth Arrow, Alfred Chandler and Herbert Simon, Coase is regarded by Williamson as one of his teachers, although that was only through the latter's publications and not through physical encounters (Williamson 1985).

uncompensated damage to surrounding woods, caused by sparks from railway engines, in the late nineteenth and early twentieth century. In Pigou's reasoning, the railway company should be forced to compensate those whose woods were burnt by the sparks from the steam engines. Coase argued that this, like many other examples of externalities from neighbours (and he cites many of them), is not just a problem of the one who harms compensating the harmed, but is reciprocal in nature. Coase (1960, p. 2) describes this as:

'To avoid the harm to B would be to inflict harm on A. The real problem that has to be decided is: should A be allowed to harm B or should B be allowed to harm A? The problem is to avoid the more serious harm.'

In other words, should the railway company be allowed to burn the woods, or should the owners of the woods be protected from sparks that could burn the woods down? The decision depends on a trade-off between the gains and the sacrifices the two property rights owners would make.

Coase goes one step further by assuming a world of zero transaction costs, in other words, that bargaining and making an agreement between two neighbours would be costless. In that situation, he argues, it would not be important who would be made liable for the damage done. The railway company and all the adjoining landowners bargain without costs until a socially optimal situation has been reached. This thesis has become very famous as the 'Coase Theorem' (a label introduced by Stigler, 1966), which Coase (1960, p. 8, 1988, p. 14), formulates as '[...] the ultimate result (which maximizes the value of production) is independent of the legal system if the price system is assumed to work without costs'. Demsetz (1967) embraces the theorem in his paper on property rights and reformulates it (though leaving the content intact) as:

'There are two striking implications of [...] a world of zero transaction costs. The output mix that results when the exchange of property rights is allowed, is efficient and the mix is independent of who is assigned ownership.'

This optimum will be reached because there would be a total trade-off, since the value of the gains and losses of each participant are known, without costs for acquiring this knowledge. Second, this trade-off would be 'on the margin', in other words the negotiators stop bargaining at a point – the margin – where there are no more gains to be made without a loss of the total (i.e. social) result.

Coase has been attacked by many for the unrealistic assumption of a world of zero transaction costs. This critique is based on a very limited knowledge or understanding of Coase's paper; he fully acknowledges that such a world does not exist. What he particularly wanted to show is the reverse of the Coase theorem. If transaction costs are zero it *does not matter* how property rights have been assigned and delineated, is the same as the statement that when transaction costs are positive it *does* matter how we have defined and attributed our property rights. To make the connection with *The nature of the firm*, without transaction costs, there would be no firms, but since there are transaction costs, they become essential organising units.

Ronald Coase has also been identified with free market environmentalism, since his emphasis on the reciprocal nature of externality problems led to the conclusion that these issues do not necessarily have to be internalised by means of government intervention. In the planning field, especially in the US, Coase has had some followers (Fischel, 1985; Ellickson, 1973; Siegan, 1972), who are very critical about zoning and make a plea for market-based arrangements for internalising externalities. In *The problem of social cost* Coase is very qualified since he makes no *a priori* or ideological decision for the governance mode. Like in *The nature of the firm*, he states that the mode of governance is dependent on the transaction. Sometimes, for instance when making an arrangement with your neighbour about reducing nuisance, it might be suitable to sign a long-term contract, instead of a more short-term and fluid market transaction. In other cases, it could be appropriate to incorporate a transaction between two parties into one organisation. There are also instances, like in the case of air pollution, which make it difficult (because of high transaction costs) to coordinate the transactions within one organisation; then government regulations (described by Coase, 1960, p. 17, as a 'very special kind of super-firm') become appropriate. Therefore, Coase does not *a priori* reject government regulations, like zoning ordinances. But he also argues that all these alternative modes of regulation are not without costs themselves. All these costs should be taken into account in what Coase calls an opportunity-cost approach, in which realistic alternatives are compared on the basis of their transaction (or opportunity) costs. This is a more realistic approach than starting – as Pigou did – from a situation of *laissez-faire* that needs to be corrected by the state. *Laissez-faire* does not exist; some even say it is planned (Polanyi, 1957). Williamson has given Coase's methodology, which he followed, the label *remediableness*. 'A condition is held to be remediable if a superior feasible alternative can be described and implemented with net gains.' (Williamson, 1996, p. 379). This replaces the concept of failure as it is often used in economics, especially in welfare economics (see also Chapter 1).

The main message of Coase in his 1960 article, is that in a world of positive transaction costs institutions matter, and more specifically, the way property rights are defined and assigned matters. This attention to property rights makes clear that we need to be more precise how we theorise about the exchange of goods and services. In the case of land: 'We speak of a person owning land and using it as a factor of production, but what the land-owner in fact possesses is the right to carry out a circumscribed list of actions.' (Coase, 1960, p. 44) Or, in other words:

'It is not the resource itself which is owned; it is a bundle, or a portion, of the right to *use* a resource that is owned. In its original meaning, property referred solely to a right, title, or interest, and resources could not be identified as property any more than they could be identified as right, title, or interest.'

(Alchian & Demsetz, 1973, p. 17)

The recognition of the importance of property rights has led to a more or less separate branch in the neo-institutional and law and economics tradition, known as the property rights approach (see also Demsetz, 1967). What is important here for the rest of the book, is that differences in the definition of property rights (on land) lead to differences in economic outcomes, of which transaction costs are a part.

To recap, the new institutional economists (e.g. Coase, 1937; Alchian & Demsetz, 1973; Williamson, 1975), unlike most old institutional economists, embraced some core ideas of neo-classical economics, like the principle of marginalism and the idea of utility maximising individuals. But they wanted to extend the applicability by considering how institutions, particularly property-rights structures, and transaction costs affect economic behaviour. They were not satisfied with the assumption of a perfectly and smoothly operating market with zero transaction costs. According to them, this cannot be applied to real-world situations. They wanted to see how economic behaviour is affected if transaction costs are not zero and how property rights affect economic actions. In the next section, I elaborate on the theme of institutions, by focusing on transactions of property rights and the norms that govern those transactions: the governance structures.

## Governance structures and property rights: building upon and refining Coase's work

John Commons introduced the transaction as a unit of analysis for economic research.

> 'Transactions are the means, under operation of law and custom, of acquiring and alienating legal control of commodities, or legal control of the labor and management that will produce and deliver or exchange the commodities and services, forward to the ultimate consumers.'                                     (Commons, 1931, p. 657)

The definition given here is slightly broader than that often used within new institutional economics. Williamson states that a transaction *'occurs when the property rights over* a good or service is transferred'* (Williamson, 1996, p. 379, my italics). What is particularly interesting in Commons' description is the word (legal) 'control', which implies that the goods or service does not need to be exchanged for attaining some degree of control. The application of zoning for instance, in this definition, can be seen as a transaction, since it is a way of increasing control over the way land is used. In the narrow (neo-institutional) sense, it would not be a transaction because there is no transfer of property rights, like for instance in the case of eminent domain or compulsory purchase. For applying transaction cost economics to planning and development, the broader definition is more suitable, since planning is about trying to control the way land is used (in the future). So, a transaction in this study should be regarded as a *legal action to increase (or take) control over property rights*. These transactions are executed – and hence control is exercised – through governance structures. In Chapters 7 and 8 especially, we will see that the quest for control over land development, and particularly the wish of public authorities to control this, significantly affects (the incidence of) transaction costs.

## Governance structures

A governance structure is 'an institutional framework in which the integrity of a transaction, or related set of transactions, is decided.' (Williamson, 1996, p. 11) Governance structures are therefore institutional arrangements that structure transactions between individuals. In new institutional economics, there is a general distinction made between institutional arrangements and the institutional environment. The former are (as already said) the governance structures (Williamson, 1990a) that guide the way economic entities interact, whereas the institutional environment is described as the legal, social and political rules that determine the context within which economic activity takes place. Williamson (1990a) takes the institutional environment as a given.

Another distinction that needs to be made here is between organisations and institutions, as these are often not precisely discussed. There has been a lot of debate within institutional research on how to deal with organisations. Are they institutions or should they be seen as something external – as agents – to those sets of rules? Some (Dequech, 2005) argue for a broad concept of institutions that encompasses organisations, since organisations are also perceived as systems of rules. This coincides with Williamson's (1975, see also Coase, 1937) treatment of the firm or public bureaucracy (Williamson, 1999), as a *governance structure*, or institutional arrangement, that is used as an alternative to the market.

For this analysis, I distinguish, like Bromley (1989) and North (1990), between institutions and organisations, regarding organisations as the 'players' that act within the institutions, 'the rules of the game'. With this distinction, firms and government agencies are treated as organisations, and hierarchical governance structures, like zoning, as institutions or institutional arrangements. However, this distinction is analytical, since they are closely interrelated in practice. Organisations are also determined by a set of rules that govern interaction within them (Dequech, 2005). Bromley (1989, p. 43) makes a distinction between the rules that govern the relationship between an organisation and the rest of the world and the rules that spell out the internal organisation. These comments could lead to the recognition that organisations are special (collective) agents and a special set of institutions at the same time (Dequech, 2005). I am mainly concerned with the institutions or rules that guide interaction between (and not within) organisations: the governance structures[5]. In general, a distinction is made between market structures, hierarchical structures and a third form, which I call relational structures. These three ideal types will be distinguished below.

**Market**

Markets have been the subject of many articles and books and hence numerous definitions circulate in economics as in the social sciences in general. Although neo-classical economists cannot understand markets satisfactorily (see e.g. Coase, 1988), due to a lack of attention to institutions and an overemphasis on explaining prices, it does not mean they have no definition of them. However these definitions are often not institutional, and regard the market as an assembly of buyers and sellers. Hirschman (1982, p. 1473) for instance, describes markets as a

> 'large number of price-taking anonymous buyers and sellers supplied with perfect information ... function without any prolonged human or social contract between the parties. Under perfect competition there is no room for bargaining, negotiation, remonstration or mutual adjustment and the various operators that contract together need not enter into recurrent or continuing relationships as a result of which they would get to know each other well.'

Coase (1988, p. 7) focuses, like most institutional economists, on the institutional nature of markets: 'Markets are institutions that exist to facilitate exchange, that is, they exist in order to reduce the cost of carrying out exchange transactions.' Hodgson uses a similar definition:

> '[...] markets involve multiple exchanges, multiple buyers and multiple sellers, and thereby a degree of competition. *A market is an institution in which a significant number of commodities of a particular, reasonably well-defined type are regularly exchanged.*'
> (Hodgson, 2002, p. 44)

---

[5] Although Alexander (1992, 2001a) has written some ground-breaking articles that have introduced transaction cost economics into planning theory, he too easily applies Williamson's framework, in which no distinction is made between organisations and institutions, to public land use planning. Alexander regards public land use planning, like for example, the firm, as hierarchical organisation. But zoning for instance, does not govern internal relations within one organisation, but relations between citizens, and between citizens and the state.

What is not apparent in Coase's definition, and gets more attention in Hodgson's description, is the element of competition, which Hirschman emphasises as well. In a classical market, or 'thick market' as Williamson (1996, p. 378) calls it, with very many buyers and sellers, there will be full competition. In cases of full competition, it is the price, which brings demand and supply in equilibrium, and therefore governs the way people transact. Individual buyers and sellers have very little influence on these market prices. A thick market is a form of governance that leaves no room for building continuing, or recurring relationships by which people get to know each other well, since it is the price mechanism that governs. The transactions between the two transacting parties, and the outcome, are not dependent on relationships, previous transactions or the identity of the actors.

This pure market form, in which personal contacts, identity or experience do not exist, is rare. The actions of individuals are embedded (Granovetter, 1985) in cultural peculiarities. In addition, in many cases there are not multiple sellers, but oligopolies or monopolies. What makes pure markets almost non-existent in the case of land exchanges and land use planning is the nature of the good 'land'. This becomes clear when we look at a part of Hodgson's definition, in which he deals with the type and number of goods that are exchanged in 'the market'. He says that in the market a *significant number of commodities of a particular, reasonably well-defined type are regularly exchanged.*' (Hodgson, 2002, p. 44). So, goods are clearly defined and regularly exchanged. But in the case of land, the word '*commodity*' hardly applies, since every piece of land is unique and immobile, which makes it almost irreplaceable by other tracts of land. In addition, the number of buyers and sellers is often limited, which leads to situations in which exchange is coordinated by mechanisms other than price, as Needham & De Kam (2004) show for the exchanges of land for affordable housing between municipalities and housing associations.

It must be noted that there are also many other broader descriptions of markets, in which exchange can take many forms (Lindblom, 2001). But for the sake of conceptual clarity, I prefer to use the relatively narrow description of the market, and I label exchanges by means other than the price mechanism such as, for instance, trust, as relational structures. Those latter governance structures will be dealt with after the market's traditional counterpart, hierarchy.

## Hierarchy[6]

Government agencies can and often do use authority (the second part of Williamson's definition) without incorporating the transaction. A good example is zoning, which is used by local authorities for various purposes (e.g. internalising externalities) without their having to own the land. McGuinness (1991) gives a good definition of hierarchy (that comes closer to this conception than Williamson's), which he regards as:

> 'a class of governance whose distinguishing feature is that a resource owner accepts restrictions (often simply because he has to) on his sole rights to use his resources in whatever way he might choose. Within those bounds of some agreed domain, he allows his resources to be controlled by an authorized decision-making unit to which he might or might not belong.'
>
> (McGuinness, 1991, pp. 74–75, parenthesis mine)

## Relational structures

One of the main criticisms of transaction cost economics has long been the dichotomy that was set up between market and hierarchy (see e.g. Coase, 1937; Williamson, 1975). But since the1980s, new institutional economists, as well as other disciplines, began to appreciate the importance of long-term contracting, hybrid governance, relational contracting, network management and the like. In public

---

[6] Since I distinguish between organisations and institutions, the firm (like Coase and Williamson do) will not be regarded as an alternative hierarchical governance structure for the market. In addition, the idea of the market and the firm as alternative structures comes from a field that mainly deals with industrial organisations. This becomes clear from Williamson's definition, when he argues that transactions are managed by hierarchies when '[...] they are placed under unified ownership (buyer and supplier are in the same enterprise) and subject to administrative controls (an authority relation, to include fiat) [...]' (Williamson, 1996, p. 378). If the costs of using the market, and buying goods, become too high, it is likely that firms decide to make the goods themselves. This became known as the 'make or buy' decision. This trade-off is hardly possible when it comes to land use decisions, since in general land cannot be made if it cannot be bought. However, the Dutch may think differently about this. As some say: 'God made the world, and the Dutch made Holland.' (Faludi, 2005). However, the 'make or buy' decision seems more applicable to serviced land in the Netherlands. Developers and housing associations choose between acquiring serviced land (which is often prepared for building by municipalities), or service land themselves.

administration, this category is usually captured under the heading 'networks' or 'policy networks' (Kickert *et al.*, 1999). However, the delineation of this category is far from clear, which can be shown by the following description:

> 'When discussing networks, in the first instance at least, it is probably institutional arrangements like *informal* groups, *mutual-aid* organizations, *small-scale* and *local institutional networks, cooperative* forms of social existence, *self-help* groups, and so on that come immediately to mind.'                                  (Thompson, 2003).

In this description, again, there is a mix of organisations and institutions. I am particularly interested in the relational arrangements *between* organisations.

Coase has argued that firms, that is, hierarchies, and markets are *alternative* modes of governance. This distinction was embraced by Williamson (1975). In Granovetter's view (1985), the way Williamson (1975) and other institutional economists, discuss the market structure is too atomistic and therefore undersocialised, and the hierarchical structure is too structuralist and therefore oversocialised. In the market, there is only room for impersonal and short term exchanges, between actors that are independent of each other and pursue their own interests. In hierarchical structures, as assumed by, for instance, Williamson, actors are subjected to an authority which they obey. Granovetter points to the difficulty of imposing authority through hierarchies and the deterministic view some have of the influence of hierarchies on individual action. The individual is not a puppet of those external social structures (Hodgson, 2000). Both these under- and oversocialised accounts neglect ongoing structures of social relations, and the embeddedness of individual action in those relationships. These social relations are essential for the (economic) actions of both people and organisations (see Putnam, 1993, 2000, Chapter 19; Granovetter, 1973)

As a reaction against the critiques of the market–hierarchy distinction, it became popular to argue that the boundaries between them are fuzzy and indistinct. New ideas like 'quasi-markets', 'hybrid forms' (e.g. Williamson, 1985) and 'internal markets' began to gain attention (Hodgson, 2002). This is the result of the observation made by many that a lot of transactions do not take place through markets (North, 1977), nor through hierarchies. In every exchange there is some implicit or explicit legal contract, leading to an exchange of property rights, but not all exchanges have the competitive and transient features that market exchanges have (Hodgson, 1988), nor the features of imposed rules or authority which hierarchies have. Hodgson (2002) calls this third category 'non-market' or 'relational' exchanges, others call it *'relational contracting'* (see e.g. Richardson, 1972; Williamson, 1985). An interesting example that I found in the pilot case (see also, Buitelaar, 2004), which preceded the cases in this study, is the informal agreement a Dutch municipality made with a large developer, which allowed the developer to develop every site in the inner city that was in the hands of the municipality. In the case studies also, in Chapters 4, 5 and 6, we will see interesting relational exchanges.

Hodgson argues that the existence of a third category should not imply that we do not need to conceptualise markets and hierarchies; the distinction between them is not blurred. Rather, there is (at least) a third distinct category: relational structures. But although markets, hierarchies and relational contracting are distinct governance structures, they can nevertheless co-exist next to each other, as we will see in the case studies.

Governance structures vary in their capacity to deal with the given circumstances (Williamson, 1985). According to Hayek (1945, 1991), it is the market structure and its price mechanism that is, most efficient in bringing about economic order. He regards cooperation between actors in this way as spontaneous. Barnard (1938) argues the opposite: that intended and induced cooperation through hierarchical structures is the most efficient mode of organising transactions. Williamson (1990b) argues that either can be most efficient in terms of transaction costs, depending on the nature of the transaction.

## How do transaction costs emerge? Transaction dimensions and economic behaviour

Arrow (1969, p. 48) defines transaction costs as the 'costs of running the economic system'. These costs have to be distinguished from the production costs, which are the main concern of neo-classical economics (Williamson, 1985). 'Transaction costs refer to all costs other than the costs of physical production [...]' (Lai, 1994, p. 84). Transaction costs emerge because we do not have perfect rationality and complete information, as is assumed in many neo-classical models. Instead, there is bounded rationality, incomplete information and opportunism. Transaction costs are the costs that are made to increase the information available to us and to reduce uncertainty. For instance, before we buy a car we try to get information about prices, quality and service. Therefore, we compare different brands and different dealers. Those activities cost time, money and effort – in other words, transaction costs.

Although the concept 'transaction costs' suggests that only the costs around a transaction are involved, it is often (as we also saw in Coase's early treatment of the concept) used more broadly. If the costs of transacting between supplier and demander are too high, one of those two might decide to incorporate the activity of the other by acquiring it from the other. For example, a car factory might decide to incorporate the activity of distributing cars, because the transaction costs of outsourcing are too high. This shift towards a hierarchical form of organisation is called vertical integration. The transaction costs might now be lower because there is no transaction. But instead of that, the organisation has the internal costs of coordinating the activity that has been incorporated. These costs are agency costs, and if these costs themselves become too high, a company may take a further decision to hive off an activity. They are often also called transaction costs. Other costs also, such as using zoning, or setting up planning agreements (like Section 106 agreements in England), which are respectively hierarchical and non-market transactions, should be seen as transaction costs. The broader definition of the transaction, which has been articulated earlier, encompasses all these activities as well.

Coase (1937) argues that a key feature of transactions is uncertainty. Uncertainty gives rise to the existence of, and changes, in organisations and institutions. He even says that 'it seems improbable that a firm would emerge without the existence of uncertainty' (Coase, 1937). Ultimately, hierarchy might be an answer to overly high uncertainty and incompleteness of contracts. Coase also said that if there are a small number of exchange relations, in which buyer and seller become dependent on each other, this too might lead to a shift to hierarchical modes of governance. Williamson (1975) felt that this line of reasoning needed to be further developed and refined. The issue of 'uncertainty' and 'small numbers' were what he called properties of the market (or *environmental factors*). They had to be connected to the *human factor*. He put forward (p. 4), two 'elementary attributes of human decision-makers': *opportunism* and *bounded rationality*.

## Economic behaviour

*Bounded rationality* is a concept that was introduced by another Nobel Prize winner, Herbert Simon (see, e.g. Simon, 1957). It acknowledges that people have a limited ability to acquire and process all the information available. People's behaviour in this respect is 'intendedly rational but only limited so' (Williamson, 1996, p. 377). So, as in most neo-classical models, the individual attempts to maximise utility, but finds it costly to do so and acknowledges his inability to anticipate all contingencies and adaptations thereto (Furubotn & Richter, 1991).

Bounded rationality in itself would not lead to many and high transaction costs if everybody was completely trustworthy. The neo-classical approach takes self-interested behaviour as a behavioural assumption on which it builds its models. But self-interested behaviour is reliable and predictable, which would not cause many (transaction) costs (incurred for anticipating that behaviour). In reality, people sometimes purposefully mislead, deceive, or otherwise confuse others. This can be placed under the word *opportunism*, which Williamson describes as 'self-interest seeking with guile'.

However, transaction costs would all be relatively low if, even with bounded rationality and opportunism, all transactions were similar and had the same characteristics. The behavioural assumptions need to be connected to an extended version of the dimensions that Coase gave to transactions. These transaction dimensions are interdependence, uncertainty and timing.

## Transaction dimensions

### Interdependence
The first of three transaction dimensions that were identified by Williamson (1985) is asset specificity. Neo-classical theories assume that resources are infinitely re-deployable and substitutable, which makes all transactions of the same goods alike. But in reality, many transactions are not recurring and only take place between a limited number of buyers and sellers. This makes these people dependent on each other. Asset specificity could be described as: 'a specialised investment that cannot be redeployed to alternative uses or by alternative users except at a loss of productive value.' (Williamson, 1996, p. 377). These investments give rise to bilateral dependency, as Williamson calls it, and will only be made if the contractors expect

a decrease in production costs or an increase in revenue. Alexander (2001a) widens this transaction dimension, by labelling it as *interdependence*, in order to go beyond the application to industrial organisation and to make it applicable to public land use planning as well. In the broader concept of interdependence, the costs of organisational and interorganisational coordination are also included. A high level of asset-specificity or interdependence might give rise to hierarchical governance structures.

**Uncertainty**

One major source of uncertainty is information-impactedness, which refers to a lack of information and/or asymmetric information (Williamson, 1975; Dixit, 1996). This could give one exchange partner an advantage over the other. The advantage might be caused by non-observability of the others' action, or pre-contract information. Williamson adds non-innocent forms of behavioural uncertainty, like opportunism, to demonstrate that not all information-asymmetries or lack of information are caused by unintentional action of the exchange partners. Some people consciously try to distort the transaction by disguising or manipulating information. Another source, which is related to information-impactedness, is complexity, which is partly attributable to interdependencies (the first dimension). The higher the uncertainty, the higher the need for uncertainty reduction, and the higher the transaction costs.

**Timing[7]**

The last of the transaction dimensions is timing, which includes the duration and frequency of transactions. This dimension is also related to the previous two. In the perfect economic market, transactions are, in principle, one-off and instantaneous exchanges. However, in reality, many transactions are not non-recurring or as speedy as these mainstream models assume. One reason might be asset-specificity or interdependence. Looking at some empirical research (Buitelaar *et al.*, 2006), we see that municipalities in the Netherlands are often committed to the same housing associations and developers. If these interchanges recur many times or continue to proceed for a relatively long time, other governance structures than the market become appropriate.

---

[7] Williamson uses frequency but, like Alexander (2001a), I prefer timing, because that encompasses both duration and frequency.

## Relationship between transaction costs and institutions

Williamson's theory is meant as a predictive theory (Williamson, 1996, p. 12). The predictive nature has become familiar under the heading *discriminating alignment*, which predicts how certain transactions will be organised or governed. This hypothesis indicates that transactions that differ in their dimensions, combined with behavioural characteristics, are aligned with governance structures, which differ in their cost and competence, in such a way as to economise on transaction costs.

Discriminating alignment makes institutions (i.e. governance structures) the dependent variable and transaction costs the independent variable. But not only do institutions respond to (potential) transaction costs, they are subject to (transaction) costs as well. These are what North (1990, Chapter 8) calls transformation costs. These transformation costs (in combination with increasing returns) are a major factor behind institutional inertia and path dependency. Coase and Williamson pay little attention to this. When various governance structures are compared, it is also the costs of making or changing these structures that need to be considered.

What is also problematic in Williamson's work, is that he takes the institutional environment as a given. The implicit assumption seems to be that governance structures are chosen rationally (albeit bounded) and independently from this environment, in order to economise on transaction costs. However, this institutional environment has an important influence on the potential governance structures at the micro-level and hence affects the transaction costs:

> 'This overall structure shapes the cost of transacting at the individual contract level, and when economists talk about efficient markets, they have simply taken for granted an elaborate framework of constraints.'                              (North, 1990, p. 66)

In planning practice, for instance, it is very difficult, or even impossible, to respond to a high degree of interdependency by introducing hierarchical governance structures. The 'choice' of the governance structure and its governance capacity is strongly dependent on the institutional and spatial context (Buitelaar *et al.*, 2006). Land ownership, past relationships between parties, planning cultures and planning legislation are just a few of the aspects of the institutional environment within which governance structures are situated and chosen. Old institutional economics pays far more attention to the wider institutional context, that is, the social, cultural and political power relationships, and their constitutive effects on the actions of agents (Hodgson, 2000), than Williamson's new institutional economics. Hodgson introduces two concepts, cumulative *downward* and *upward causation*, which show much resemblance to the ideas behind Giddens' duality of structure (Giddens, 1984). Individuals create and change institutions (upward causation), just as institutions mould and constrain individuals (downward causation). Therefore, institutions do not have a once-for-all influence, but are continuously constructed and reconstructed in an ongoing process of interaction (Granovetter, 1985, p. 486).

Williamson emphasises the ability of actors, individually and atomistically, to shape governance structures so as to maximise their utility. Granovetter (1985) labels this emphasis on voluntaristic design, and the lack of attention for social structures, as 'undersocialisation'. On the other hand, there is also a danger of structural determinism, which Granovetter describes as 'oversocialisation'. Structures may influence the actions of agents; it does not mean that they determine their behaviour.

The problem, however, with duality of structure, is that it conflates agents and structures entirely (Hodgson, 2004). In Giddens' view, 'structure... is internal to actors' (Hodgson, 2004, p. 33). But this neglects the fact that there can be structures at different levels. There are some structures that are not constructed by the present actors but, for instance, exist at higher (or different) structural levels or by virtue of past generations of actors. To give an example, the real estate market, or the *structure of building provision* (Ball, 1998), can be influenced relatively little by the actions of individual stakeholders in a redevelopment project.

The use of governance structures and the related transaction costs are embedded in an institutional context. This context could also be seen as the 'culture' within which actions are taken, if culture is defined as 'the sum of and the interrelationships among institutions' (Neale, 1994). These institutions can be, and often are, a mixture of both formal and informal institutions. In (new) economic sociology (Granovetter, 1985; Callon, 1998; Abolafia, 1998) and old institutional economics (e.g. Hodgson, 2004)[8], much more attention has been given

---

[8] New economic sociology and old institutional economics have so many similarities that it is surprising to see how little cooperation takes place between them (Velthuis 1999).

to the relationship between culture and economic actions. Recently, this combination of sociology and economics has also gained ground in property research (Guy & Henneberry, 2000; Guy *et al.*, 2002). This book, in line with those just mentioned, links the actions in the development projects to the other (i.e. higher) level structures.

Therefore, I make a distinction between different institutional levels, following the distinction made by Alexander (2005) for institutional analysis in planning research. These are specified and related to each other in Figure 2.1. Alexander makes a distinction between macro, meso and micro institutions. At each level we find both formal and informal institutions. Micro-level institutions are the rules that shape the interaction between individuals and organisations. In this research, these are Williamson's governance structures. Their construction and use leads to transaction costs in the development process. These governance structures are, however, not constructed out of an infinite range of alternatives. The focus is particularly on how formal institutions are constructed. There are institutions at the meso level that limit the possibilities. These meso-level institutions form the rules of

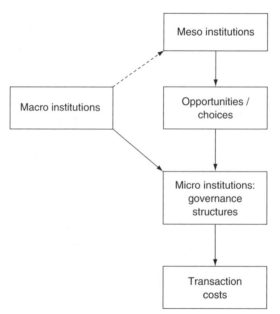

**Figure 2.1**   Conceptual framework of institutions and transaction costs.

the game that different actors face when entering into development practices. This level includes '[...] incentives and constraints in the form of laws, regulations and resources to develop and implement policies, programs, projects and plans.' (Alexander, 2005, p. 214). Examples are planning and building laws, financial incentives (like the Planning Delivery Grants in England), land policy practices, etc. This meso-level constrains (or enables) the actions in the development process to some extent, but (as said before) it does not determine or dictate them. There is a lot of room for agents to manoeuvre. In addition, the way agents act is often embedded – though again not determined – in a system of social and cultural norms and values, which I define as the macro-level institutions[9].

It needs to be noted that the terms macro, meso and micro are only used for the sake of labelling and structuring the text. There are also significant disadvantages in using them, like any other distinction. For instance, the different levels are separated from each other arbitrarily; in practice the boundaries are blurred and the levels largely conflated. In addition, the headings macro, meso and micro imply a top-down hierarchy, while the relationship between the institutional layers is reciprocal (and therefore all arrows in Figure 2.1 should also point in the reverse direction). However, in this study I am mainly interested in how transaction costs in the development process are produced, and therefore how the interplay between agents and institutions at different levels affect the actions, and the transaction costs that result from that, at the micro level. In Hodgson's terms, the emphasis is therefore more on 'cumulative downward causation' than on 'upward causation'.

The conceptual framework just presented is not yet completely applicable for the empirical field of planning and development. In Chapter 3, the right part of Figure 2.1 – starting from the meso level down to transaction costs – will be discussed by operationalising it for land use decisions. After the operationalisation, it will be applied to the case studies in Chapters 4, 5 and 6, followed by a comparison in Chapter 7. Four important elements of the institutional macro level are derived from the case studies and additional literature, which will be elaborated by additional empirical research in Chapter 8.

---

[9] Obviously, the macro and the meso level are also interrelated, but this relationship gets less attention in this study. Therefore, the arrow is dashed.

# References

Abolafia, M. Y. (1998) Markets as cultures: an ethnographic approach. In: M. Callon (ed.), *The Laws of the Market*. Blackwell, Oxford.

Alchian, A. A. & Demsetz, H. (1973) The property right paradigm, *The Journal of Economic History* **33**(1): 16–27.

Alexander, E. R. (1992) A transaction cost theory of planning, *Journal of the American Planning Association* **58**(2): 190–200.

Alexander, E. R. (2001a) A transaction-cost theory of land use planning and development control. Toward the institutional analysis of public planning, *Town Planning Review* **72**: 45–75.

Alexander, E. R. (2001b) Why planning vs. markets is an oxymoron: asking the right question, *Planning and Markets* **4**(1).

Alexander, E. R. (2005) Institutional transformation and planning: from institutionalization theory to institutional design, *Planning Theory* **4**(3): 209–23.

Arrow, K. J. (1969) The organization of economic activity: issues pertinent to the choice of market versus nonmarket allocation, in: (eds.), *The Analysis and Evaluation of Public Expenditure: The PPB System*, pp. 59–73. US Government Printing Office, Washington DC.

Ball, M. (1998) Institutions in British property research: a review, *Urban Studies* **35**(9): 1501–17.

Barnard, C. (1938) *The Functions of the Executive*. Harvard University Press, Cambridge MA.

Bradach, J. L. & Eccles, R. G. (1989) Price, authority, and trust: from ideal types to plural forms, *Annual Review of Sociology* **15**: 97–118.

Bromley, D. W. (1989) *Economic Interests and Institutions*. Blackwell, Oxford.

Buitelaar, E. (2004) A transaction-cost analysis of the land development process, *Urban Studies* **41**(13): 2539–53.

Buitelaar, E. (forthcoming) Zoning: more than just a tool. Explaining Houston's regulatory practice, *Journal of Planning Education and Research*,

Buitelaar, E., Lagendijk, A. & Jacobs, W. (2007) A theory of institutional change: illustrated by Dutch city-provinces and Dutch land policy, *Environment and Planning A* **38**.

Buitelaar, E., Mertens, H., Needham, B. & De Kam, G. (2006) *Sturend Vermogen en Woningbouw: Een Onderzoek Naar Het Vermogen Van Gemeenten Om Te Sturen Bij De Ontwikkeling Van Woningbouwlocaties*. DGW/NETHUR, Den Haag/Utrecht.

Callon, M. (1998) Introduction: the embeddedness of economic markets in economics, in: M. Callon (ed.), *The Laws of the Market*, pp. 1–57. Blackwell, Oxford.

Coase, R. H. (1937) The nature of the firm, *Economica* **4**: 386–405.

Coase, R. H. (1960) The problem of social cost, *Journal of Law and Economics* **3**: 1–44.

Coase, R. H. (1984) The new institutional economics, *Journal of Institutional and Theoretical Economics* **140**: 229–31.

Coase, R. H. (ed.) (1988) *The Firm, the Market and the Law.* The University of Chicago Press, Chicago IL.

Commons, J. R. (1931) Institutional economics, *American Economic Review* **21**(4): 648–57.

Cooter, R. & Ulen, T. (2004) *Law & Economics.* Pearson Addison Wesley, Boston MA.

Demsetz, H. (1967) Toward a theory of property rights, *The American Economic Review,* **57**: 347–59.

Dequech, D. (2002) The demarcation between "old" and "new" institutional economics, *Journal of Economic Issues* **36**(2): 565–72.

Dequech, D. (2005) Institutions: a concept for a theory of conformity and innovation. unpublished paper.

Dixit, A. K. (1996) *The Making of Economic Policy: A Transaction-Cost Politics Perspective.* MIT Press, Cambridge MA.

Ellickson, R. C. (1973) Alternatives to zoning: covenants, nuisance rules, and fines as land use controls, *The University of Chicago Law Review* **40**: 681–781.

Faludi, A. (2005) The Netherlands: a culture with a soft spot for planning. In: B. Sanyal (ed.), *Comparative Planning Cultures,* pp. 285–307. Routledge, New York.

Fischel, W. A. (1985) *The Economics of Zoning Laws.* The Johns Hopkins University Press, Baltimore MD.

Furubotn, E. G. & Richter, R. (1991) The new institutional economics: an assessment. In: E. G. Furubotn & R. Richter (eds.), *The New Institutional Economics: A Collection of Articles from the Journal of Institutional and Theoretical Economics,* pp. 3–32. Mohr, Tübingen.

Giddens, A. (1984) *The Constitution of Society.* Polity Press, Cambridge.

Granovetter, M. (1973) The strength of weak ties, *The American Journal of Sociology* **78**(6): 1360–80.

Granovetter, M. (1985) Economic action and social structure: the problem of embeddedness, *The American Journal of Sociology* **91**(3): 481–510.

Guy, S. & Henneberry, J. (2000) Understanding urban development processes: integrating the economic and the social in property research, *Urban Studies* **37**(13): 2399–416.

Guy, S., Henneberry, J. & Rowley, S. (2002) Development cultures and urban regeneration, *Urban Studies* **39**(7): 1181–96.

Hamilton, W. H. (1919) The institutional approach to economic theory, *American Economic Review* **9**(1): 309–18.

Hayek, F. A. (1945) The use of knowledge in society, *American Economic Review* **35**(4): 519–30.

Hayek, F. A. V. (1991) Spontaneous ('grown') order and organized ('made') order, in: J. F. G. Thompson, R. Levacic & J. Mitchell (eds.), *Markets, Networks & Hierarchies: The Coordination of Social Life,* 293–301. Sage Publications, London.

Hazeu, C. A. (2000) *Institutionele Economie: Een Optiek op Organisatie – en Sturingsvraagstukken.* Uitgeverij Coutinho, Bussum.

Hirschman, A. O. (1982) Rival interpretations of market society: civilizing, destructive, or feeble, *Journal of Economic Literature* **20**: 1463–84.

Hodgson, G. M. (1988) *Economics and Institutions: A Manifesto for a Modern Institutional Economics.* Polity Press and University of Pennsylvania Press, Cambridge/Philadelphia PA.

Hodgson, G. M. (2000) What is the essence of institutional economics? *Journal of Economic Issues* **34**(2): 317–29.

Hodgson, G. M. (2002) The legal nature of the firm and the myth of the firm-market hybrid, *International Journal of the Economics of Business* **9**(1): 37–60.

Hodgson, G. M. (2004) *The Evolution of Institutional Economics: Agency, Structure and Darwinism in American Institutionalism.* Routledge, London.

Kickert, W. J. M., Klijn, E.-H. & Koppenjan, J. F. M. (eds.) (1999) *Managing Complex Networks: Strategies for the Public Sector.* Sage, London.

Lai, L. W. C. (1994) The economics of land-use zoning. A literature review and analysis of the work of Coase, *Town Planning Review* **65**: 77–98.

Lindblom, C. E. (2001) *The Market System. What It Is, How It Works and What to Make of It.* Yale University Press, New Haven CT/London.

McGuinness, T. (1991) Markets and managerial hierarchies, in: J. F. G. Thompson, R. Levacic & J. Mitchell (eds.), *Markets, Networks & Hierarchies: The Coordination of Social Life.* Sage, London.

Neale, W. (1994) Institutions, in: G. Hodgson, W. Samuels & M. Tool (eds.), *Companion to Institutional and Evolutionary Economics.* Edward Elgar, Aldershot.

Needham, B. & De Kam, G. (2004) Understanding how land is transacted: markets, rules and networks, as illustrated by housing associations, *Urban Studies* **41**(10): 2061–76.

North, D. C. (1977) Markets and other allocation systems in history: the challenge of Karl Polanyi, *Journal of European Economic History* **6**: 703–16.

North, D. C. (1990) *Institutions, Institutional Change and Economic Performance.* Cambridge University Press, New York.

Pierre, J. (1999) Models of urban governance: the institutional dimension of urban politics, *Urban Affairs Review* **34**: 372–96.

Pigou, A. C. (1920) *The Economics of Welfare.* Macmillan, London.

Polanyi, K. (1957) *The Great Transformation.* Rinehart, New York.

Posner, R. A. (1993) The new institutional economics meets law and economics, *Journal of Institutional and Theoretical Economics* **149**(1): 73–8.

Putnam, R. D. (1993) *Making Democracy Work, Civic Traditions in Modern Italy.* Princeton University Press, Princeton NJ.

Putnam, R. D. (2000) *Bowling Alone: The Collapse and Revival of American Community.* Simon & Schuster, New York.

Richardson, G. B. (1972) The organisation of industry, *Economic Journal* **82**: 883–96.

Siegan, B. H. (1972) *Land Use Without Zoning.* Lexington, Lexington MA.

Simon, H. (1957) *Administrative Behavior.* Macmillan, New York.

Smith, A. (1904 [1776]) *An Inquiry into the Nature and Causes of the Wealth of Nations*, 5th edn. Methuen, London.

Stigler, G. J. (1966) *The Theory of Price*. Macmillan, New York.

Thompson, G. F. (2003) *Between Markets & Hierarchies: The Logic and Limits of Network Forms of Organization*. Oxford University Press, New York.

Veblen, T. B. (1899) *The Theory of the Leisure Class: An Economic Study in the Evolution of Institutions*. Macmillan, New York.

Velthuis, O. (1999) The changing relationship between economic sociology and institutional economics: from Talcott Parsons to Mark Granovetter, *American Journal of Economics and Sociology* **58**(4): 629–49.

Williamson, O. E. (1975) *Markets and Hierarchies*. Free Press, New York.

Williamson, O. E. (1985) *The Economic Institutions of Capitalism: Firms, Markets, Relational Contracting*. Free Press, New York.

Williamson, O. E. (1990a) Chester Barnard and the incipient science of organization, in: O. E. Williamson (ed.), *Organization Theory: From Chester Barnard to the Present and Beyond*, pp. 172–206. Oxford University Press, New York.

Williamson, O. E. (1990b) A comparison of alternative approaches to economic organization, *Journal of Institutional and Theoretical Economics* **146**: 61–71.

Williamson, O. E. (1993) Transaction cost economics meets Posnerian law and economics, *Journal of Institutional and Theoretical Economics* **149**(1): 99–118.

Williamson, O. E. (1996) *The Mechanisms of Governance*. Oxford University Press, New York.

Williamson, O. E. (1999) Public and private bureaucracies: a transaction costs economics perspective, *Journal of Law, Economics and Organization* **15**: 306–42.

# 3

# Operationalising Institutions and Transaction Costs

This chapter deals with the operationalisation of institutions and transaction costs for the empirical study. In the empirical research, the central question posed in Chapter 1 has been addressed: how are the different institutional levels and transaction costs interrelated under different circumstances, and how does this affect the existence, size and incidence of transaction costs in the development process? To answer this we need an analytical framework that can be applied to identify institutions and transaction costs in land development, under

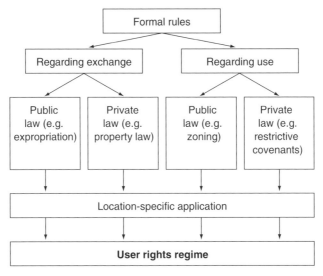

**Figure 3.1** *User rights regime* (combination of Buitelaar, 2003 and Segeren *et al.*, 2005).

different circumstances; that is, on different sites, in different cities, in different countries. In other words, it is a framework that has general applicability for democratic systems of land use decision-making. In this chapter the focus is particularly at the micro level, which means that the concepts of governance structures and transaction costs are operationalised. But the relation with the meso level will also be made (e.g. in Figure 3.1), since meso-institutions limit the options at the micro level. First, the concept of user rights regimes is introduced as a specific governance structure. A method for identifying transaction costs is also described, especially for those costs that are related to the creation and the use of the user rights regime. Furthermore, the choices for the empirical research are set out and explained.

The approach followed in this study differs slightly from earlier approaches, most notably that of Ernest Alexander. His approach is *normative*, while I want to use a more *analytical and explanatory*[1] perspective. After Williamson (e.g. 1999), Alexander uses the term *discriminating alignment*, which means that transactions and their dimensions (interdependence, uncertainty and timing) are aligned with alternative governance structures. In the case of what are called 'idiosyncratic transactions' – with their high interdependence and uncertainty, repetition and long duration – firms or public bureaux (that is, hierarchy) are the appropriate forms of governance. Alexander uses transaction cost theory normatively, since it provides prescriptions for institutional design. I want to analyse development processes and the institutional arrangements within these processes, identify transaction costs, their size and distribution and find explanations. This makes the approach more analytical and explanatory. What makes the methodology of 'discriminating alignment' less suitable is the narrow demarcation of the transaction (and its dimensions), that is, as an *exchange* of

---

[1] Explanatory in this sense means trying to explain the existence, size and distribution of transaction costs. It does not mean transaction-cost minimising explanations for institutions and institutional change, as is often done in new institutional economics (see e.g. Demsetz, 1967; Williamson, 1985). I regard the indication of (the minimisation of) transaction costs and efficiency as driving forces behind institutional change as too functionalistic and based on the assumption of rational acting individuals (see also Buitelaar, 2004). As others (Ball, 1998; David & Han, 2004) have said, the empirical validity of this explanatory version of transaction costs economics is to be questioned. Other approaches like sociological institutionalism and discursive institutionalism (e.g. Hajer, 1995) seem more valuable on this point (Buitelaar *et al.*, 2007). In the latter, explanations for institutional change are found in changes in discourse.

property rights, as explained in Chapter 2. The transaction, as the unit of analysis, is defined more broadly in this study. The dimensions' interdependency, uncertainty and timing are primarily related to the narrow definition, and are therefore less easily applicable to an empirical study that seeks to identify transactions in land development and land use planning.

## User rights regimes as particular governance structures[2]

After Alexander (and therefore after e.g. Williamson, 1996), I use the transaction as the unit of analysis, since it is a ubiquitous, concrete and well-defined unit (Alexander, 2001a, p. 48). However, in the way in which Alexander uses it, this unit is not sufficient to cover the whole range of institutional arrangements through which land use is changed. I use Commons' broader definition of a transaction, which is expanded to acquiring legal control over property rights; this is therefore broader than acquiring control by obtaining the property rights. In Chapter 2, I defined, in line with Commons, the transaction as a *legal action to increase (or take) control over property rights*. Governance structures have been defined as 'an institutional framework in which the integrity of a transaction, or related set of transactions, is decided.' (Williamson, 1996, p. 11). Governance structures are the means to increase or change control over property rights.

With regard to land use and land use decisions, it is the right to use, rather than the question who has the right to 'full ownership', that is central[3]. Other parts of the bundle of property rights, like the right to income or the right to transfer are less important (or are purely instrumental) for land use planning, although they are very much related to the right to use. When we apply the three governance structures (market, hierarchy and relational structures) to land use planning issues, we examine how they are used to *deal with changes in land use by changing the ownership or the content of user rights*. This needs to be explained further. If someone wants to change the use of

---

[2]  A large part of this section is derived from Buitelaar (2003).

[3]  The bundle of rights consists of the right to use (*usus*), the right to income (*usus fructus*) and the right to transfer (*abusus*) (De Alessi, 1991). 'It is the bundle of rights that society recognizes as ownership' (Jacobs, 1998, p. x).

the land to which he owns the user rights, he can usually do that by exercising his rights. But governance is about adjusting, influencing and regulating the actions of *other* owners of user rights. Suppose that a person (or an agency) wants to change or influence the use of land to which he does not possess user rights. He can do this either by acquiring the user rights or by taking actions that change the content of the user rights. The three governance structures above can be used to do either.

Applied to land use, we can distinguish a *market* in user rights. In market forms of governance, someone buys the whole bundle of property rights on a piece of land, or just the user rights or part of the user rights. People can 'buy their way out of an externality problem' by buying (parts of) user rights in order to prevent externalities. This idea is based on the work of Coase (1960). For example, a factory is next to a forest. The factory emits toxic gasses that are harmful to the forest. The owner of the forest and the owner of the factory can take account of these externalities through exchange of a part of the user rights. The question is: how much is a 'clean' forest environment worth, in terms of money, to the forest owner, and how much is a full emission, through which the factory can produce maximally, worth to the factory owner? If the forest owner is prepared to compensate the factory owner for polluting the air to a lesser extent, for example, by compensating the factory owner for closing down a part of the factory, he actually buys a part of the user rights of the factory owner. Through this transaction the forest owner decides partly about the use of the land of the factory owner[4]. Obviously, if the forest owner buys the whole right to use the land on which the factory is built, or the whole bundle of property rights (with the user rights included), he decides about the full use of it. There is an important difference between transacting a *part* of the user rights and transacting *all* the user rights or the *whole* bundle. The difference is that buying parts of the user rights (like the forest owner did) changes the content of user rights (of the factory owner). Buying all the user rights or the whole bundle of property rights does

---

[4] It must be noted here that there is a fine line between market and relational structures. Given the definition of markets in Chapter 2, as being structures that facilitate transitory, non-recurring and non-relational exchanges, it must be said that most (or almost every) exchange of parts of the user rights are not market exchanges. If we look at the example of the factory, it is unlikely in the case of land that people who enter into exchanges have no relationship, since they are often neighbours.

not change the content of the user rights but just the ownership of the user rights[5].

When hierarchy is applied to the governance of land use, land use *planning* by a public agency is the main form seen (Alexander, 1992, 2001a). As the definition of McGuinness (1991, see also Chapter 2) shows, in hierarchical forms of governance, it is someone or something else other than the owner of the user rights that decides about the attenuation[6] or transfer of the user rights on a piece of land. The best known example of attenuation of user rights is zoning. Expropriation goes further; now the content of the user rights (and the other rights too) is not attenuated, but the user rights together with the rest of the rights within a bundle of rights are transferred. The user rights are not changed, but the ownership is. For zoning the opposite is true.

Good examples of relational contracting in the case of land use are public–public, private–private or public–private partnerships, which are voluntarily entered into. Another example is the agreements developers and planning authorities reach about public facilities (like Section 106 agreements in England). Such partnerships and agreements can be bilateral as well as multilateral, and between neighbouring property owners as well as between other stakeholders (like the municipality) and the property owners. Relations are not only used for changing the content of the user rights, but also for changing the ownership of the user rights. Needham & De Kam (2004) show that Dutch housing associations do not only acquire their land 'through the market', but also (often below the market price) with the help of municipalities. Another example of relational forms of governance directed to changing the ownership of user rights is land readjustment on a voluntary basis by neighbouring property owners. There are also combinations in which both the content and the transfer of user rights is arranged. In the Dutch case we will see such an example of what is called a development agreement.

---

[5] It must be noted that pure markets as defined in Chapter 2 do not or rarely exist, since exchanges are generally relational to some degree, especially in the case of exchanges between neighbours.

[6] If we start from absolute ownership, a landowner is entitled to do with his property whatever he wants '... from a parcel's horizontal boundaries, ever upward to the heavens and ever downward to the depths' (Ellickson, 1993, p. 1363). Every action by the government that restricts the exercise of this principle must be seen as an attenuation of property rights.

In (almost) every democratic country there are rules from both public law and private law regarding land exchange and land use. In Chapter 2, these could be seen as the rules of the game at the meso level. Private law consists of the general rules that are set up to facilitate exchange (not only with regard to land) between citizens. Under private law we find, among other things, property law and contract law. Examples of applications of these private rules are development agreements (see Chapter 4), restrictive covenants (see Chapter 6) and easements (Chapters 5 and 6). Public law comprises the rules that arrange the relationship between the citizen and the state, and between government agencies, like national planning acts or acts on compulsory purchase. These general laws get local application, for instance in the case of zoning, development control, expropriation and so on. In every development process, these public and private law rules are created and/or used differently. The site-specific application that concerns the right to use a particular piece of land is what I call the user rights regime for that land. This will be the core object of the transaction-cost analysis.

## A transaction-cost analysis of the development process: a methodology

'Transaction costs' is a broad concept that needs to be further specified. First, there are the costs of acquiring information; in the case of land use planning this could be, for example, a research into residential preferences. These transaction costs are called *information costs*.

Uncertainty can be (and often is) reduced by using institutions. Property rights on land, for instance, means that there are rights and consequently (see Bromley, 1991) duties with respect to a particular piece of land. These reduce uncertainty about what can and cannot be done with that land, and by whom. North (1990a, p. 3) defines institutions as: '[...] the rules of the game in a society or, more formally, [...] the humanly devised constraints that shape human interaction.' Institutions are *created* or changed, after which they are *used*[7]. The creation and use

---

[7] Sometimes creation and use coincide. For instance, with designing the Town & Country Planning Act in the UK in 1947, the development plan as an institution was *created*. If the local government makes a development plan it *uses* the Town & Country Planning Act and at the same time *creates* local rules that have to be taken into account when planning permission is decided upon.

(see for this distinction Furubotn & Richter, 1991, p. 8) of institutions involve costs – transaction costs, or more specifically *institutional costs*.

The advantage of this more dynamic and less deterministic view on institutions is that the 'duality of structure' (Giddens, 1984; Healey & Barrett, 1990), that is, the difficulty of separating structure and agency when it comes to explaining social behaviour, is incorporated. The word 'creating' shows that institutions are 'humanly devised constraints' (North, 1990, p. 3), that is, social constructions, and 'using' (or acting within) institutions shows that on the other hand that institutions 'shape human interaction' (North 1990, p. 3). With this approach it is not necessary, or even appropriate, to distinguish between the transaction costs that are caused by agencies using the institutions and the transaction costs that are caused by agencies when they make these institutions: these are interwoven.

In Figure 3.2, I have summarised the different costs of the development process in order to specify the concept of transaction costs. This study focuses on the costs of creating and using institutions, more specifically the user rights regimes. The costs of acquiring information independent of the institutional arrangements, if there are any, are what I call the information costs.

Transaction costs are rarely measured (Furubotn & Richter, 1991). If they are at all quantified, they are usually put as a non-specified item on an account, for example, 'administrative costs'. In addition, as we will see in the coming chapters, many transaction costs are only indirectly related to the development process. Therefore, transaction costs are not measured in this study. Here, I put forward a methodology for *identifying* transaction costs (see also, Buitelaar, 2004).

To identify transaction costs, and particularly the costs that can be attributed to a user rights regime, the development process forms an appropriate time frame, since it is within this process that a user rights

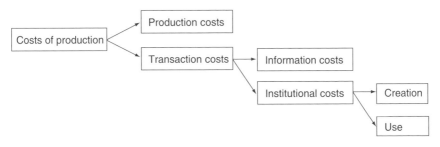

**Figure 3.2**   Specifying the costs of the development process.

regime is created and used. Healey (1992, p. 36) defines land development processes as:

> '[...] the transformation of the physical form, bundle of rights, and material and symbolic value of land and buildings from one state to another, through the effort of agents with interests and purposes in acquiring and using resources, operating rules and applying and developing ideas and values.'

The development process can be regarded as a sort of production process[8]: on a particular location the built environment is changed, that is produced. The production process in a supply chain has been approached from a neo-institutional economic perspective (see e.g. Williamson, 1975, 1985). The development process of the built environment can also be analysed from a transaction-cost perspective. Healey's definition also shows that creating and using institutions is an integral part of the transformation process of one land use to another.

It is important to distinguish transaction costs from production costs. I use the model of the neo-classical market as point of reference to make the distinction. The difference, it is often argued, between neo-classical economics and new institutional economics is the lack of attention for institutions and transaction costs in the former (e.g. Eggertson, 1990; North, 1990). A neo-classical market is assumed to function smoothly and without friction. 'Property rights are perfectly and costlessly specified and information is likewise costless to acquire' (North, 1990, p. 11; North also argues, p. 17, that although few economists believe that behavioural assumptions reflect human behaviour, they build many models upon these same assumptions). This leads to a situation where there are only production costs and no transaction costs. So, if we want to carry out a transaction-cost analysis, we must ask the question: would the costs that we find also be found in a neo-classical development process? If the answer is 'yes', then they are production costs, if the answer is 'no', they are transaction costs.

---

[8] Although the analogy with the production process is made, I do not intend to focus on capital flows and their determining role in the development process, and human interaction in general, as in many Marxist production-based models of the development process (Gore & Nicholson, 1991; Healey, 1991). In addition, production-based models hardly take account of the role of institutions. The analogy simply emphasises the supply side of development (see also, Van Der Krabben, 1995).

This sounds too simple, but it will become clear that this is a very useful way to approach all the activities in the development process. I will give an illustration. The costs that contribute directly to building a house are the production costs, these costs would also have to be made in a frictionless neo-classical 'world'. The other costs are the transaction costs, which have to be made because of the acquisition of information, or the creation and use of institutions. To give an example, the acquisition of land would also be an activity that is needed in a neo-classical 'market'[9]: if you want to build a house you need land. So, the price of land is a production cost. But negotiation and contract-making around the acquisition of land would not have existed in a frictionless market, and are therefore transaction costs. Another example is the making of a building plan. A design is a necessary activity in the production process of a house or a housing block, also in the neo-classical model. The deliberation about the design between the municipality and the developer, in order for the developer to get planning permission, is part of the transaction costs, as are the costs of the negotiation between the developer and the architect.

I focus on the transaction costs (and their size) that are the result of the creation and use of the user rights regimes[10]. User rights regimes play an important role in several occasions in the development process. I distinguish four such occasions in Table 3.1. These four stages have not been chosen randomly. A pilot case study, other empirical research

**Table 3.1**   Moments/stages in the development process where the user rights regime is created and/or used.

1. Land exchange
2. Making land use or zoning plan/building ordinance etc. (that is, regulations of land use)
3. Agreement (between for example, developer and municipality)
4. Planning permission

[9] It should be noted that, because a price has to be paid for a piece of land (like any other good), it suggests that there is an institution like private property; while a neo-classical market is supposed to be 'institutionless'.

[10] I must add to this that the change and use of institutions do not only give rise to the transaction costs, but can also increase the production costs. For instance, the application of some environmental act might require soil decontamination. These costs are production costs, but do not exist in a neo-classical market. So, transaction costs are the costs (other than the production costs) that would not exist in a neo-classical market, not being the costs of the *physical* production of the built environment. I will give no further attention to the latter costs.

(like Verhage, 2002) and the first experiences with the cases that can be found (see Chapters 4, 5 and 6) in this book have shown that it is in these four stages in the development process that the user rights regime is created and/or used. I argue that this approach is applicable to most Western countries and, in general, those countries that at least have the institution of 'private property', surrounded by rules from the property rights regime, often supplemented with rules (under public law) that regulate land use.

The first category is that of land exchange, which deals with the transfer of property rights, more specifically user rights, of a piece of land. Before land is transformed from one land use in another, it is often exchanged, for instance from a farmer to a developer or from a local authority to a housing association. There can be several exchanges of the same piece of land. The second stage in the development process where the user rights regime is involved is in the making of a land use or zoning plan. In most (but not all) local authorities in Europe and the US, local land use plans are made to indicate and prescribe conditions for the location and nature of land use development. These conditions demarcate the boundaries of the user rights. Obviously, costs are involved with this. Thirdly, the category 'agreement' has been identi-fied. Agreements can be both statutory (like the Section 106 agree-ment in England) and non-statutory, such as restrictive covenants or public–private partnerships. These agreements can be used (and often are) to mutually agree upon the demarcation of the user rights. The last category in Table 3.1 is 'planning permission' (or building permit), which could be seen as *using* the user rights regime. Here planning applications are judged more (as in the Netherlands) or less (in England) on the basis of the user rights regime. This exercise also involves time, money and effort.

Assumptions have also been made about what kind of variables within each of the four categories might give rise to transaction costs. Those have been addressed in Table 3.2. These factors are neither meant as hypotheses that will be proven or rejected in the end, nor as an exhaustive list, but are intended to aid and guide the empirical research. Here again, a pilot case, knowledge from secondary sources and the first experiences in the case study research have resulted in this list of variables. The four moments/stages do not only involve costs in themselves, but influence the duration of the development process as a whole, and the costs related to this. These related costs include inter-est costs that rise over a longer duration.

**Table 3.2** Possible transaction-cost influencing factors with creating and using the user rights regimes (see also, Buitelaar, 2004).

| Moments/stages in the development process where the user rights regime is created and/or used | Possible transaction-cost influencing factors |
|---|---|
| 1. Land exchange | – number of parties involved and the number of parcels exchanged<br>– conflict of interest<br>– information about future possibilities<br>– delineation (assignment) of rights<br>– and the information of the delineation of rights: land registry or not<br>– use of hierarchical means (for example, compulsory purchase, pre-emption rights) |
| 2. Making land use or zoning plan/building ordinance etc. (that is regulations of land use) | – stakeholder participation<br>– appeal<br>– number of parties involved<br>– conflict of interest<br>– structure of the plan: legally binding – indicative<br>– structure of the procedure: administrative – political |
| 3. Agreement (between, for example, developer and municipality) | – number of parties involved<br>– conflict of interest<br>– structure of agreement/contract: detailed – flexible |
| 4. Planning permission | – yes, no, or conditional<br>– number of parties involved<br>– conflict of interest<br>– possibility of negotiation (planning gain)<br>– possibility of appeal and the actual use of it<br>– structure of the procedure: administrative – political<br>– structure of the permission: conditional – unconditional |

Land exchanges are facilitated by rules from the user rights regime. Using these institutions involves costs. The costs might be further determined by how rights are delineated, the information about that, knowledge about future possibilities, the number of parties that want to acquire the land and whether or not hierarchical measures like compulsory purchase can be or are being used.

Factors related to the plan-making stage (if there is a plan) that generate transaction costs, could include the structure of the plan-making procedure and the plan, stakeholder participation, the number of stakeholders, conflict between them and appeal possibilities and use.

In some development processes, agreements such as restrictive covenants or (the British) planning agreements are signed by different parties to influence or determine the exercise of the user rights. Again, for the size of the transaction costs, the number of parties and their conflicts will be important, as well as the structure of the agreement (detailed versus broad).

The last category is the planning permission. Not every system (as we will see) has a land use plan and planning permission. But if it does, it is important to know whether it is a political or administrative procedure, whether the permission is conditional or unconditional, if there is room for negotiation or appeal, how many parties are involved and whether their interests conflict. It should be clear that the empirical analysis does not include an analysis of the costs of creating the relevant acts (at the meso-level). This is considered part of the institutional context or environment.

## The empirical research

The framework that has been built in Chapter 2 and particularly Chapter 3, has been applied to different case studies in different countries. Case study research is an appropriate method for conceptually complex and empirically intensive studies. The relationship between institutions, and between institutions and transaction costs, is complex, due to many types of institutions at different levels, with loops between them. In addition, transaction costs are often numerous, diverse and non-transparent. This requires a labour-intensive research method.

Cases in several countries have been chosen, because the assumption is that the relationships that I want to reveal differ under different circumstances, as the central question also indicates. For that reason, comparing them in different countries is most interesting, since the meso-level institutions – public and private law with regard to land use – can differ significantly between countries. In the case of planning law, each site has its own site-specific application, but that does not mean that country-specific limitations are not important. The differences between different sites within one country might be great, but the differences between national legislation, and the institutional context in general, could make the differences between sites (in different countries) even greater.

Another choice I have made is for *one* type of development process, namely the development of a small housing site. The reason for choosing one type of development process is that this reduces the number of variables. Comparing different kinds of projects with different property rights regimes and different spatial planning regimes, becomes more complex and probably impractical (Buitelaar, 2003) and so I have chosen to keep the output of the development processes (a small housing site) constant. Therefore, different housing projects in different countries with a similar number of houses, similar housing densities, and similar division of social and commercial housing and so on, have been chosen. Obviously, there will still be differences between different sites. But as Verhage (2002, p. 36) argues: 'However, without trivialising these differences, we can also argue that we see much the same. Although the details are different, we are walking on a sidewalk. We are looking at buildings situated in gardens. Along the road are parking places, and if we look up we see street lighting. Although we may tend to focus on the differences, a lot of the things we see are the same as they are in our own country. To notice these similarities we need a certain level of abstraction.'

Transaction costs, as already said, are often numerous. Large housing sites are often complex and therefore involve many transaction costs. For this reason, I have chosen to compare *small* housing sites. An additional difficulty is that transaction costs are often indirect and therefore hard to indicate. An example is a local authority that employs a consultant for drawing a land use plan, who might decide to buy the expertise of an urban designer or a lawyer. With all these parties involved and the related costs, it becomes difficult to track down all these (indirect) transaction costs. To get a comprehensive picture of all the transaction costs and to compare as many cases as possible, smaller sites (around 100 houses) are more suitable.

The cases are 'Marialaan' in Nijmegen (The Netherlands), 'Wapping Wharf' in Bristol (England) and 'Montebello' in Houston (Texas, USA). The countries or states have been chosen for the differences in meso-level institutions, primarily for the differences in planning systems. The Dutch system is based on the principle of legal certainty, with a prominent role for the legally binding *bestemmingsplan*. In the English system, discretion plays a much greater role, and therefore the development plans (and, since the system change in 2004, the Local Development Frameworks), have a less prominent and a more indicative role. In Texas, cities are not obliged to have zoning ordinances and plans, and Houston is one of the few that decided not to adopt these. It therefore has no zoning, and it is generally considered to be a city with a market-based planning system. Houston, however, is not the free market city it is often claimed to be (Larson, 1995)[11]. Many other plan-ning regulations are in place and legal certainty is an important ele-ment of those rules. In short, the role of the plan (or lack thereof) and the balance between certainty and flexibility are quite different in the three countries. The assumption is that this affects the choice of user rights regimes and the transaction costs related to them. This 'choice' is not only dependent on the meso-level institutions, but is also embedded in social and cultural structures at the macro-level. Again, it must be noted that the institutional distinction and the labels (macro, meso and micro) are analytical and arbitrary. The main macro level institutions are identified (empirically) from the case studies and additional literature. This is done at the end of Chapter 7 and elabo-rated empirically in Chapter 8.

The projects – Marialaan, Wapping Wharf and Montebello – have been chosen for practical reasons. Important considerations were access to the information, they had to be recently completed and they had to comprise apartment complexes/condominiums of around 100 units to make them comparable. They are not meant to represent the way development is carried out in each country, although they are not peculiar in their country. The cases have their own development and their own site-specific characteristics.

In the different cases, both content analysis and interviews (see Appendix A) have been used to acquire primary information about the sequence of the events, the involvement of stakeholders and especially about the way the user rights regimes was created and used. I have paid particular attention to the two most important parties in the develop-ment process, namely: the developer and the municipality. Content analysis looked at policy documents, land use plans, agreements, plan-ning permissions/building permits and correspondence between stake-holders, most notably between the municipality and the developer. These documents were provided both by files from local authorities and by files from the developer or the architect. The interviews were held with the responsible agents from the side of the developer and case officers within the local authorities. The first step was the reconstruction

---

[11] In that sense El Paso (in Texas near the border with Mexico) would be a better example of a market system, but due to the absence of building regulations, subdi-vision and infrastructure requirements, residential conditions, infrastructure and sewerage are poor (Larson, 1995). That makes this case difficult to compare to other cases, in which more or less the same result is produced with different institutional arrangements.

of the process in order to get an overview of the sequence of events. The next step was to trace the determinants behind the transaction costs that can be attributed to the user rights regime. It should be noted that the exposition of the information is not exhaustive, since it has not always been possible to obtain all the necessary sources, for reasons such as confidentiality and incompleteness of files. The additional empirical research for Chapter 8, directed to explore the embeddedness of transaction costs in macro-level structures, is based on policy documents, secondary literature, and interviews with practitioners in strategic and management positions, and with academics (see also Appendix A).

The next three chapters are empirical, each covering one country. The sequence of the chapters is the same as is the sequence in which the case studies have been carried out. First, a brief introduction is given about some basic features of the property rights and planning regime. Then a description is given of the development process in the particular case. Finally, a transaction-cost analysis of each of the development processes is made. After this is done for each country, an aggregated analysis and comparison is made in Chapter 7.

# References

Alexander, E. R. (1992) A transaction cost theory of planning. *Journal of the American Planning Association*, **58**(2): 190–200.

Alexander, E. R. (2001a) A transaction-cost theory of land use planning and development control. Toward the institutional analysis of public planning. *Town Planning Review*, **72**(1): 45–75.

Ball, M. (1998) Institutions in British property research: a review. *Urban Studies*, **35**(9): 1501–17.

Bromley, D. W. (1989) *Economic Interests and Institutions*, Blackwell, Oxford.

Bromley, D. W. (1991) *Environment and Economy: Property Rights and Public Policy*. Blackwell, Cambridge MA.

Buitelaar, E. (2003) Neither market nor government. Comparing the performance of user rights regimes. *Town Planning Review*, **74**(3): 315–30.

Buitelaar, E. (2004) A transaction-cost analysis of the land development process. *Urban Studies*, **41**(13): 2539–53.

Buitelaar, E., Lagendijk, A. & Jacobs, W. (2007) A theory of institutional change: illustrated by Dutch city-provinces and Dutch land policy. *Environment and Planning* **A**, **39**(4): 891–908.

Coase, R. H. (1960) The problem of social cost. *Journal of Law and Economics*, **3**: 1–44.

David, R. J. & Han, S.-K. (2004) A systematic assessment of the empirical support for transaction cost economics. *Strategic Management Journal*, **25**(1): 39–58.

De Alessi, L. (1991) Development of the property right approach. In: E. G. Furubotn & R. Richter (eds.), *The New Institutional Economics: A Collection of Articles from the Journal of Institutional and Theoretical Economics*. Mohr, Tübingen.

Demsetz, H. (1967) Toward a theory of property rights. *The American Economic Review*, **57**(2): 347–59.

Eggertsson, T. (1990) *Economic Behaviour and Institutions*. Cambridge University Press, Cambridge.

Ellickson, R. C. (1993) Property in land. *The Yale Law Journal*, **102**: 1315–400.

Furubotn, E. G. & Richter, R. (1991) The new institutional economics: an assessment. In: E. G. Furubotn & R. Richter (eds), *The New Institutional Economics: A Collection of Articles from the Journal of Institutional and Theoretical Economics*. Mohr, Tübingen, pp. 3–32.

Giddens, A. (1984) *The Constitution of Society*. Polity Press, Cambridge.

Gore, T. & Nicholson, D. (1991) Models of the land-development process: a critical review. *Environment and Planning A*, **23**(5): 705–30.

Hajer, M. A. (1995) *The Politics of Environmental Discourse: Ecological Modernization and the Policy of Process*. Oxford University Press, Oxford.

Healey, P. (1991) Models of the development process: a review. *Journal of Property Research*, **8**: 219–38.

Healey, P. (1992) An institutional model of the development process. *Journal of Property Research*, **9**: 33–44.

Healey, P. & Barrett, S. M. (1990) Structure and agency in land and property development processes. *Urban Studies*, **27**(1): 89–104.

Jacobs, H. M. (ed.) (1998) *Who Owns America?: Social Conflict Over Property Rights*. The University of Wisconsin Press, Madison WI.

Larson, J. E. (1995) Free markets deep in the heart of Texas. *The Georgetown Law Journal*, **84**(2): 179–258.

McGuinness, T. (1991) Markets and managerial hierarchies. In: J. F. G. Thompson, R. Levacic & J. Mitchell (eds.), *Markets, Networks & Hierarchies: The Coordination of Social Life*. Sage, London.

Needham, B. & De Kam, G. (2004) Understanding how land is transacted: markets, rules and networks, as illustrated by housing associations. *Urban Studies*, **41**(10): 2061–76.

North, D. C. (1990) *Institutions, Institutional Change and Economic Performance*. Cambridge University Press, New York.

Segeren, A., Needham, B. & Groen, J. (2005) *De Markt Doorgrond. Een Institutionele Analyse van Grondmarkten in Nederland*. RPB/NAi Uitgevers, Den Haag/Rotterdam.

Van der Krabben, E. (1995) *Urban Dynamics: A Real Estate Perspective. An Institutional Analysis of the Production of the Built Environment* (dissertation). Thesis Publishers, Amsterdam.

Verhage, R. (2002) *Local Policy for Housing Development: European Experiences*. Ashgate, Aldershot.

Williamson, O. E. (1975) *Markets and Hierarchies.* Free Press, New York.

Williamson, O. E. (1985) *The Economic Institutions of Capitalism: Firms, Markets, Relational Contracting.* Free Press, New York.

Williamson, O. E. (1996) *The Mechanisms of Governance.* Oxford University Press, New York.

Williamson, O. E. (1999) Public and private bureaucracies: a transaction costs economics perspective. *Journal of Law, Economics and Organization,* **15**(1): 306–42.

# 4

# Nijmegen: The Quest for Control in a Corporatist Tradition

In this chapter, I describe the Dutch case study (see Section 'The Marialaan case: small but complex'), which is a housing site in the city of Nijmegen. This case could be seen as typical for the way the Dutch carry out development projects. There is an active involvement by the municipality and it took over 8 years to deliver the output. The main reason that it took so long was the amount of deliberation within the municipality and between the municipality and the developer. In the Section ('Transaction-cost analysis of the Marialaan') after the description of the development process, a transaction-cost analysis will be made. But before that, a general picture needs to be sketched ('Dutch planning and property law') of the legal system in general, of the property and planning systems in particular, of the way Dutch municipalities are involved in land development and the kind of tools they have for that.

## Dutch planning and property law

Neither property nor planning law is designed and applied in a vacuum, but they are parts of a wider legal and administrative context. Newman & Thornley (see, e.g. 1996), following Zweigert & Kötz (1987), distinguish between various legal families so as to indicate different legal styles of groups of countries. The Netherlands is considered as being part of what is called the 'Napoleonic' family. This family, to which France, Belgium, Spain, Portugal and Italy also belong, has a tendency to use abstract legal norms (often formulated in a constitution) and to have legal debates about them, more than is the case in the 'British' family which is more pragmatic, and based on a case by case (evolutionary) approach. There is an inclination in the Napoleonic family to think things through in advance, mainly to set up a clear system that provides legal certainty. This has also become known as the 'rule of law' (see, e.g. Moroni, 2005). The abstract legal norms are translated into a system of rules, both in private law (like the civil code) and in public law (like a national planning act). We will see examples of the first when property law is discussed and examples of the latter when the national planning act and the tools for land acquisition (like compulsory purchase and pre-emption rights) are discussed.

What distinguishes the Netherlands from other countries also in the Napoleonic family, is the state structure and especially the relationship between the different layers of this structure. The state structure consists of three layers, the municipal, the provincial and the national level. The Dutch see their system as a 'decentralised unitary state'. This combines features of German local autonomy and French centralism (Faludi, 2005). In the case of planning, legally the centre of gravity is at the local level, which has the only plan which is legally binding, the *bestemmingsplan*. The plans at the provincial and national level are strategic indicative plans, with very few legally binding elements. However, there are some ways[1] in which the higher tiers of government can intervene in the local level. In addition, financially, the centre of gravity is at the central level, and 80% of municipal funding comes from central government. This has led to a 'fused system' (Newman & Thornley, 1996), in which responsibilities (and power) are divided among the levels and agencies of government, which makes it difficult (though not impossible) for agencies on each level to autonomously decide and carry out their own policies. (This is different to the English situation where the central government and local authorities have more of a principal–agent relationship.)

Because the core of this book is about the way rules with regard to land use are created and applied, we need a good understanding of the way property and statehood are defined in the Dutch context. Booth (2002a) makes an interesting comparison between the origins of law in continental Europe and English law. As we will see in the next

---

[1] For instance, the municipal *bestemmingsplan* has to be approved by the province. Another example is the possibility that provinces and the central government have to give a directive if the local planning policy is not in accordance with the national or provincial policy.

chapter, English property law is based on the two foundations *benefi-cium* and *feudum*, while European systems are built on two concepts from Roman law, namely *dominium* and *imperium*.

## Dominium: property rights

Dominium represents the exclusive right of the owner to the current use and the future development of an entity. This is also known as absolute ownership. This contrasts with feudal systems, in which the existence of multiple interests in a piece of land is a key feature. Absolute ownership is central in Dutch property law. Although property is not defined in the Constitution (while expropriation is), it is defined by law in the civil code. Two of the most important phrases that demonstrate the exclusive beneficial enjoyment of property are: 'property is the most encompassing right a person can have on a thing' (Section 1, part 1, book 5 BW, civil code), and on the use of property: 'the owner is free to use his property, with exclusion of others, as long as this use is not incompatible with rights of others, and pays attention to legislation and justified restrictions based on unwritten law' (Section 1, part 2, book 5 BW, civil code).

Although property is defined and protected in law, legal ownership of land never had the same symbolic value as it has in many other countries, like the US (Jacobs, 1998). The process in which land ownership became subordinate and instrumental to societal values has been called the 'socialisation of ownership' (Van Den Bergh, 1979; Teijmant, 1988). The value of land ownership is more instrumental than ideological, since it is treated as a policy variable to carry out spatial objectives. Land acquisition by the state is generally acknowledged, as well as government restrictions on the way landowners use their property. The fundamental discussions that are held in the US on the question of when restrictions should be seen as 'regulatory taking' are largely absent in the Netherlands.

## Imperium: planning law[2]

The sole and undisputed right to property nests within a system that gives the state the right to intervene in the landowners' rights for the

---

[2] At the moment of writing this, the WRO is being revised. The new situation is not yet clear. But what is clear already is that the initially intended fundamental revision has become far less fundamental.

benefit of the general public, based on an idea of imperium. Imperium refers to the right of the state to govern individual actions. In Dutch public law, the state provides different government layers, and especially the local level, with all sorts of tools that can be applied to influence land use.

The core of the Dutch planning system is formed by the planning act (Wet op de Ruimtelijke Ordering, abbreviated as WRO) in conjunction with the housing act (Woningwet). The Dutch development control system is known as a limited-imperative system, which is quite similar to the French system (Booth, 1996), and which is based on the rule of law tradition. 'Limited' means there are a limited and known number of conditions (based on Section 44 of the housing act) to which a building application must comply. Imperative means that these conditions are legally binding. If an application meets these conditions, permission has to be granted, and if it does not, the municipality is required to reject it. However, in the latter case, the municipality can use various exemptions to deviate from the stipulated conditions. The housing act says that a building application can only be, and should be, rejected if it does not meet the conditions set in the national building code, the local building ordinance, the land use plan (*bestemmingsplan*), the monument act, and a review by the municipal design committee.

The *bestemmingsplan*, which is close to a zoning plan, is especially important in this research. It is made at the local level by municipalities, which have the discretion to decide whether they want a broad plan, a detailed plan, or a plan that is initially broad but will be further specified within a prescribed time frame (Section 11, WRO). In many cases (especially when housing is concerned), in order to keep control, municipalities decide to make detailed plans. Often applications from developers do not fit into these tight plans. In these situations, the municipality should reject the applications, unless it wants to grant an exemption from the existing plan. There are various types of exemptions. There are 'in-plan' exemptions, which means that the particular *bestemmingsplan* can prescribe under which circumstances and conditions the municipality can deviate from it. There are also temporary exemptions that allow for departures from the plan for a five-year period, and a possible extension of another five years (Section 17, WRO). The most famous section in the WRO is Section 19, which has three subsections. Section 19.1 is widely used to allow major developments to proceed without having to change the *bestemmingsplan* immediately. Although the procedure is not fast, it is shorter than the procedure for making a new plan. Section 19.2 is used for a series of activities and functions that are enumerated by the province in which the locality is situated. And finally there is Section 19.3 that can be used for the small deviations from the *bestenmmingsplan.*

Although the system is designed to provide legal certainty for both civilians and government agencies, practice shows a more pragmatic picture. Because *bestemmingsplannen* are inert to change, they are generally not changed in order to plan in advance, but more to confirm already (informally) approved development. Municipalities are obliged by law to renew a plan after ten years, but because there is no sanction for not doing this, the country is covered by many plans that are well over ten years old. The advantage for local authorities is that new private development initiatives often do not fit into these older plans (see also the Marialaan); this is an advantage because otherwise the authorities might have to grant permission whether they like it or not. If the application is not in line with the conditions, which is more likely with older plans, the developer asks the local authority to deviate from its own legal regime. This gives the municipality an important power position in relation to the developer. In order to facilitate the development and change the (user rights) regime, local authorities can then impose conditions to the developer. This is an important practice for municipalities to achieve their goals when they do not own the land themselves.

**Land policy and public tools for acquiring land**
For many years now the Dutch have celebrated the motto that 'who owns the land, builds' (Overwater, 2002). In the Netherlands, land development (that is, producing serviced building plots) and property development are often separated due to a dominant role in the land market by municipalities. In many countries both activities are carried out by real estate developers. Active land policy as a means to achieve policy ambitions is an important feature of planning practice (Needham *et al.*, 1993). As we will see, this is quite different from practice in Bristol and Houston, and in England and the US in general. Although public land acquisition is under pressure, in 2000, municipalities still possessed the majority of the land for development, namely 64% of the Vinex (named after the national policy memorandum, published in 1993, that designated various big sites in or near urban areas for development) locations and 68% of the other locations (Korthals Altes & Groetelaers, 2000).

Active land policy involves land assembly and land development by the municipality, after which it often sells off the land for property development to private developers or housing associations. This tradition has persevered for many decades now (De Kam, 1996, p. 222). After World War II, a massive programme for subsidised housing had to be implemented, for which the government took the initiative. The result of this programme is that the Netherlands now has the highest percentage of social housing in Western Europe. Active land policy by municipalities was necessary to implement this programme.

Nowadays, the percentage of social housing is decreasing and the number of subsidised houses built annually is far less than it used to be in the 1960s and1970s. However, active land policy has retained much of its importance. One could say that after World War II, the institutionalised practice of active land policy has always been supported by a hegemonic discourse, that is, active state involvement in the production of space, despite the emergence of other discourses, like privatisation, since the1980s – as in many other countries. Municipalities stick to active land policy for two reasons primarily. The first reason is the grip on spatial development that this gives to the municipality. In general, the planning system, as laid out in the Dutch spatial planning act (WRO) and building act, does not provide sufficient means to achieve the ambitions of the local government. In a way, it is a negative system that prohibits some land uses and hence allows others. To implement policy and to achieve the ambitions, a more active strategy is needed.

The second reason is the financial benefit the municipality can gain from this active policy, which it uses because of its limited range of options (due to the centralised financial system) to levy taxes or otherwise increase income. With active land policy, the financial profits in the development process can be collected by the municipality, instead of 'leaking away' to developers and housing associations. In addition to getting the income, the municipalities can recoup plan costs and the costs of services such as public space, social housing and infrastructure. Unlike the English planning system with its *planning obligations*, or the American growth management with its *concurrency* (a 'pay-as-you-grow' strategy), the Dutch formal system is not capable of recouping the above mentioned costs. Again, in the Dutch system certain land uses can only be prohibited, nothing can be imposed. It is for these two reasons that municipalities use active land policy. After the land has been developed, it is often sold off with conditions on future land use. This can give municipalities far-reaching control over development.

Besides privately acquiring land, and in this way acting as a 'normal' market participant, local governments can use public hierarchical tools in cases where land owners do not want to sell voluntarily. The first is compulsory purchase, as we know it in many other countries. Expropriation does not occur much, because the procedure is time- and money-consuming. The tool is mainly used as a threat behind 'voluntary' land transfers. Another tool that helps to reproduce active land policy as a convention is the use of pre-emption rights, which is regulated in the *Wet Voorkeursrecht Gemeenten* (WVG, which can be literally translated as 'Municipal Pre-emption Rights Act'). This act gives the municipality the right to first refusal of acquisition of a piece of land in a designated area, in case of a proposed transaction by the initial landowner. When the landowner wants to sell his land and the municipality has imposed a pre-emption right, the land owner is obliged to offer the land first to the municipality. In the next section, we will see in action some of the instruments just mentioned.

## The Marialaan case: small but complex

The Marialaan project (more precisely, stage 1) is an urban renewal project in the western part of the city of Nijmegen, a city in the east of the Netherlands (near the German border), which has around 160 000 inhabitants (it is the 10th city in the Netherlands, as of 1 January 2005). The project was completed in 2003, and includes 96 apartments, 1550 m$^2$ commercial space and parking underneath. Before the land was converted into the current land use, it was in two parcels, one occupied by a gas station and the other by a builders' merchant.

The Marialaan project is part of an area that became known in municipal circles as the MVK triangle, which is the area between the Marialaan, Koekoestraat and Voorstadslaan (see Figure 4.1). The official project start was in 1994. A developer (called KDO) together with an association of retailers in that area commissioned a 'development perspective' to explore the potential for redevelopment of the MVK triangle. The municipality endorsed the main points of this document and agreed to cooperate actively in redeveloping the area. This decision was also informed by a shopping survey that was commissioned by the municipality a year before the development perspective (in 1993),

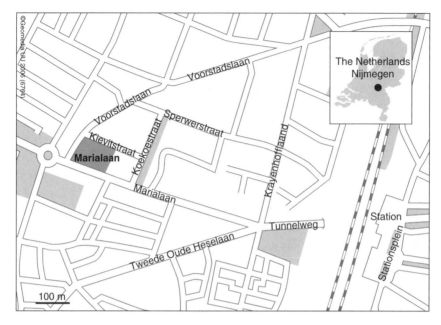

**Figure 4.1**    The Marialaan project © Geomedia UU 2006 (6764).

which stated that the retail structure was one-sided, meaning too many big retailers (such as supermarkets). In addition, the particular site was run down, while at the same time the area around it had become part of an urban renewal scheme.

When the municipality showed willingness to cooperate, KDO decided to start negotiations with the landowners. KDO signed a provisional sales contract for the northern part, with the owner of the site (T&L vastgoed – the owner of the land on which two super-markets and one big clothing store operated) in 1995. But it was clear that a long and difficult negotiation trajectory had to be followed to close the contract. Therefore, early on in the process the triangle was split into two parts (and hence two projects), the part south of the Kievitstraat – the Marialaan project – and the area north of it. The Marialaan project itself was further divided in two stages. This chapter will be about stage 1, the area that was previously occupied by the builders' merchant and the gas station. Stage 2 is east of stage 1, which is also part of the area south of the Kievitstraat. A car repair business and a pharmaceutical producer occupied that area. Currently, this area is being redeveloped.

In 1995, the land of the gas station was acquired by KDO. The land was seriously contaminated and had to be cleansed. When land is contaminated, a decontamination plan has to be made, which has to be based on a soil report. The plan and the report were made by December 1996 and approved by the province in June 1997, after which the cleansing works could start (above a certain size of contaminated land – 25 m³ – the province becomes the appropriate public agency for decision making). These were accomplished in 2001 and KDO paid 122 000 Euros for the decontamination.

The acquisition of the builders' merchant by KDO proved to be unfeasible. Initially, the municipality stated that KDO was responsible for the land acquisitions. But when KDO said this was not possible, the municipality made some calculations, early in 1995. On the basis of a residual land price method, a cost-effective development was possible if a maximum of 450 000 Euros was paid for the land. However, the value of the land under its existing land use (as a builders' merchant) was higher than under the proposed land use. This made land acquisition unprofitable and hence impossible for KDO. Therefore, the municipality of Nijmegen decided to buy the land. It arranged with the owner to exchange the location for another location (both plots appraised at a value of 730 000 Euros each) without additional payment. The old plot was slightly contaminated, but not as much as the site of the gas station. Both the decontamination plan and the decontamination itself were paid for by the original landowner. In July 2001 the site was cleansed.

Eventually, the negotiations with the owner of the northern side of the MVK triangle (T&L Vastgoed) ran aground. Some of the stakeholders (KDO and the municipality) said that the price that the landowner was asking was exceptionally high. The municipality tried in vain to mediate and to rebuild trust between the parties. But KDO decided to stop the negotiations and to devote its attention exclusively to the Marialaan project. It took a long time for another developer to be able to buy the land outside the Marialaan project, which happened in January 2004. One of the reasons that the acquisition was successful later, was the positive spin-off from the first stage of the Marialaan project. The houses there were sold quickly.

Parallel to the land acquisitions for the Marialaan project (stage 1), around 1995, the municipal requirements for development – the planning brief – were being made. On the basis of the development perspective, the municipality (together with the developer) set the (design) conditions under which it was willing to cooperate and change the existing legally binding land use plan. The existing plan had to be changed because developer KDO proposed to build houses, while the plan only allowed retail, car repair or infrastructure. In the initial conditions, a reservation was made for 57 apartments. After the conditions were approved by both parties, they jointly selected an architect who was asked to draw up a provisional design, taking into account the conditions that the municipality enumerated. The municipality agreed to bring a new *bestemmingsplan* into procedure when the provisional design had been approved. Soon after the start, due to a lack of progress in acquiring the rest of the area, it was decided that the *bestemmingsplan* would cover only the first stage of the MVK triangle: the Marialaan project.

In December 1995, some first sketches were made in order to start the discussion. A year later, in December 1996, a first draft design was finished and subjected to discussion by a working group consisting of people from various municipal departments (like public space, traffic and transport, building and housing, strategic policy and water engineering) and some representatives of KDO. It took some time to come up with a draft design, after the conditions had been approved, because initially the municipality also involved a housing association to see whether a proportion could be built as social housing. After various calculations, all parties decided that was not feasible and the housing association withdrew. In addition, the existing composition of the neighbourhood – the majority of the people had low incomes – led to the decision that it would be good to attract higher income groups as well.

The working group debated the various draft designs until January 1998, when the (definitive) draft design was handed to the design committee (*welstandscommissie*) for review. A month later a public meeting was held in which the neighbourhood was informed about the joint plan of the municipality and the developer. There were two major objections against the scheme. One was about the height and the volume of the structure. The people living on the Voorstadslaan – which is directly opposite the building – would lose a lot of sun light in their gardens. The other problem raised in the meeting was the lack of parking space in the plan and the problems that that could cause for the neighbourhood. In May that year (1998) the architect drew a new design in which some of the floors at the side of the Voorstadslaan were removed and garage was included to deal with the parking issue. Obviously, these changes raised costs and cut income. To cover this, the prices per apartment were increased.

A new draft design with fewer storeys and a garage was yet again sent out for public consultation. The reactions were moderately positive. A third (definitive) draft design was made to account for some minor comments. This was the 'real' final version, which was satisfactory for all stakeholders and would form the basis for the *bestemmingsplan* procedure. This document was subjected to formal public consultation in March 1999. It was adopted by the municipal council in December 1999 and approved by the province in March 2000, which made a total of one year for the *bestemmingsplan* procedure. During this formal procedure there was not much objection from the neighbourhood. Otherwise it could have taken a lot longer.

When the *bestemmingsplan* was brought into action, the department of project management had to officially commission a plan for the public space (at a price of 120 000 Euros) to the department of city maintenance. At the same time, KDO had to elaborate its plans in more detail in order to prepare for applying for a building application, after the *bestemmingsplan* was approved.

Parallel to the various sketches, designs and plans (starting as of December 1995), a discussion was initiated about a joint land servicing account (which contains all the costs and benefits of producing service building plots), and more particularly about the division of costs between the developer and the municipality. This process took approximately four years, till November 1999, when an intention agreement was signed by both parties. They decided to make the agreement because in the preceding years not much, or only slow, progress had been made, and because they both felt the need for something more tangible to fall back on. At the same time, some changes had to be made to the initial calculations because of the addition of the earlier mentioned garage and the decrease in the number of units. In August 2000, a development agreement, or exchange contract, was signed in which both parties, in line with the intention agreement, exchanged building land – from the municipality to the developer – and land for public space – from developer to the municipality – with each other. The developer had to pay the municipality 349 000 Euros, which comprised the land price – 730 000 Euros – of the parcel of the builders' merchant land that the municipality had previously acquired, plus process costs made by the planning department and the municipal land agency of 130 000 Euros, plus the costs of the soil research of 2300 Euros, plus the costs of the notary of 1900 Euros, minus a national urban renewal subsidy of 515 000 Euros that the municipality used for this project.

After the building had been constructed, all the apartments were quickly occupied. It took longer for all the commercial space to be let. The Marialaan project served, and still serves, as a catalyst for redeveloping adjacent run-down areas.

## Transaction-cost analysis of the Marialaan

Nijmegen, like most municipalities in the Netherlands, reserves a sum of money for the transaction costs, or 'VTA'[3] it expects to make. When municipalities make a land servicing account (grondexploitatie), they generally (Van Hoek, 2004; Nijland, 2005) reserve for their own transaction costs around 25% of the costs of preparing the land for building. In the Nijmegen case, this included the costs of running the *bestemmingsplan* procedure up to the approval of the plan by the province, because the plan had to be changed to make development possible. It did not include testing the application for the building permit. In the case of the Marialaan, the municipality decided to recoup 130 000 Euros by including it in the land price the developer had to pay to the municipality. In the last project calculation (in the file) of the property specialists of the municipality, the real process costs were calculated as 166 000 Euros. But because an agreement with the developer had already been made, an additional 36 000 Euros were borne by the city. When we look at Table 4.2, these costs consist of the costs associated with the acquisition of land from the builders' merchant, preparing a design that was suitable for the *bestemmingsplan* procedure, negotiation and deliberation before the decision to make an intention agreement, costs of setting up the intention agreement, making the development agreement and land exchange contract, and the formal procedure of the *bestemmingsplan*. More specifically there were various disciplines involved as part of the VTA costs: those of the man-hours of civil engineers, the environmental costs (both research and mediation itself), urban designers, legal department (for the formal procedure), city maintenance department (for the public space), and the costs made by the municipal land department (project management, planning & control, land acquisitions and financial managers).

---

[3] In the Netherlands, there are many abbreviations to indicate those costs, such as VAT, VTU, V&T etc.

**Table 4.1**   Transaction costs on the balance sheet of the developer.

| | |
|---|---|
| Fees planning permission | 134 000 € |
| General advice | 10 000 € |
| Legal advice | 5500 € |
| Cost calculations | 3400 € |
| Unanticipated costs | 14 700 € |
| Total | 167 600 € |

Beside the transaction costs that were 'imposed' by the requirements of the municipality, the developer obviously also made its own costs. On the building account of the developer (see Table 4.1) there are only some marginal items that can be seen as transaction costs, like the costs that had to be paid to external parties – such as the fees to the city and the consultancy costs. In addition, there are costs that have been indicated as unanticipated costs. Although these can also be seen as production costs, in the sense that they have been used for physical works, they have been made because there was no complete certainty in advance, which make them transaction costs.

In Table 4.2 we can see the activities associated with creating and using the user rights regime. In many cases, like the preparation of the plan and the preparation of the agreement, events evolved simultaneously.

## Land exchange

What is typical of the way in which Dutch municipalities pursue land policy, is their active involvement from the very beginning of the development process. What is rare in most other countries, but fairly common in Holland, is the financial contribution which the municipality made (of 1360 Euros, against a contribution of 910 Euros by the developer) to the development perspective (in 1994) that was made to asses the development potential of the site.

The parcels of land in the first stage of the MVK triangle – of the gas station and the builders' merchant – were relatively easy to acquire. KDO acquired the gas station within a couple of months and the municipality did the same for the land owned by the builders' merchant, when it became clear (early on) that the developer could not do this profitably. The nature of the property rights on the land, in terms of demarcation and clarity, did not cause many extra costs.

**Table 4.2**    Transaction costs at the Marialaan.

| Activities | Indication of the amount | Borne by |
|---|---|---|
| **1. Land exchange** | | |
| Acquisition of land of the builders' merchant | Around six months | Municipality |
| Acquisition of the gas station | Few months | Developer |
| Sale of the apartments | – Establishing apartment rights: 4100 Euros<br>– Notary costs: 57 000 Euros<br>– Brokerage: 112 000 Euros | Developer |
| **2. Land use or zoning plan** | | |
| Preparing a design that was suitable for the *bestemmingsplan* procedure | From the start in November 1994 till October 1998 | Developer and municipality (but because of recoupment mainly the developer) |
| *Bestemmingsplan* procedure | 1 year (March 1999– March 2000) | Primarily by the municipality, but recouped from the developer (130 000 Euros) |
| **3. Agreement** | | |
| Negotiation and deliberation before the decision to make an intention agreement | From the start in November 1994 till March 1999 | Municipality and developer (large part of the municipal costs is recouped from developer) |
| Intention agreement | From first to final version – 8 months | Municipality and developer (large part of the municipal costs is recouped from developer) |
| Development agreement and land exchange contract | From first to final version – 9 months | Municipality and developer (large part of the municipal costs is recouped from developer) |
| **4. Planning permission** | | |
| Demolition permission | | Municipality and developer |
| Preparation for planning permission | Consultancy hired by KDO: 19 000 Euros | Developer mainly |
| Planning permission | 13 weeks<br>Costs: 3200 Euro for municipality fees: 134 000 Euros | Municipality, but more than covered by the developer through the fees |
| Inspection | Part of the 3200 and 134 000 Euros | Municipality, but more than covered by the developer through the fees |

The selling of the apartments by KDO was also a straightforward activity. The main costs that were made were the 'default' costs of every development that is sold by a developer such as: the costs of establishing apartment rights of 4100 Euros, the notary costs of 57000 Euros, but also marketing costs (50000 Euros) and brokerage (112000 Euros). The costs of the apartment rights, the notary costs and brokerage should be seen as costs related to the user rights regime. Their relationship with the user rights regime is clear and direct. But there are also costs that are more indirect.

One of the indirect costs that could be identified is that resulting from the difficulty of acquiring the land of the northern part of the MVK triangle. Compulsory purchase is difficult and costly. In addition, expropriation must be based on a planning regime that supports it, which was not yet the case, since at that time the *bestemmingsplan* still designated the area for another land use. Therefore, the developer and the city decided to split the area. This probably almost doubled the process costs, because two land use plans had to be made, two development agreements had to be negotiated, and so on.

Another indirect cost resulting from the way the city dealt with the land acquisition, was that originating from the 'choice' to find a replacement site for the builders' merchant elsewhere in the city. One could argue that the costs of actively facilitating this are a result, on the one hand, of the fact that the municipality pursued an active land policy (which is a way of using the user rights regime) and on the other hand a result of not using expropriation (and not being able to). This is understandable because of the difficulty with, and the limitations on, compulsory purchase. However, it is part of the way the user rights regime is used and created.

It needs to be said that the transaction costs of land exchange from the municipality to the developer and vice versa could also be put under the 'land exchange' heading, but since it is linked to a development agreement, in which the municipality included several requirements for the developer as well, it is classified under the agreement Section (number 3).

## Land use or zoning plan

Because the *bestemmingsplan* had to be changed in order to allow houses to be built, the municipality could take the opportunity to be closely involved in determining the conditions under which development could occur. This led to an extensive process of deliberation between the developer and the city of Nijmegen. However, because of its position, the municipality was able, to a large extent, to require the developer to pay the process costs that the municipality incurred during the process.

It is difficult to distinguish between the minimum costs of a design and the actual costs of making (and discussing) the design, and hence there is mix of production and transaction costs. In addition it is difficult, or even impossible, to distinguish between the costs that were incurred in the drawing and discussing of the plans, and the costs incurred in signing an agreement/contract over this plan (category 3). It took four years from the development perspective in November 1994, until the draft design in October 1998. This was mainly used for discussion and deliberation between municipal agencies, the municipality and the developer and for public consultation. Various designs and various calculations were made to support these plans. Altogether, the city of Nijmegen estimates its own process costs (including the costs of discussing the design and preparing the agreements) at round 166 000 Euros. But again, it needs to be said that although this consists primarily of transaction costs, in the strict sense some of the costs should been seen as production costs.

Then there is the time that was used for the formal procedure of the *bestemmingsplan*. In the existing legislation the maximum number of weeks for a *bestemmingsplan*, before it has become irreversible, is 110 weeks, just over two years. In this case, it took nearly a year from the moment it was subjected to formal public consultation (since there had been some informal meetings in the neighbourhood before) to the moment that it became irreversible.

Nijmegen has around 600 *bestemmingsplannen* at the moment, many of them are so-called 'postage stamp plans'. Many of these are very small plans that include only few plots. The *bestemmingsplan* for the Marialaan, which previously counted only two relatively small parcels, is one of those plans. Because the acquisition of the northern part of the MVK triangle was laborious, the municipality decided to include in the new *bestemmingsplan* only the first stage of the Marialaan project. It was too risky to include to the whole MVK triangle, since changing a plan later due to a change of views or other cause, leads to an extensive revision procedure. *Bestemmingsplannen* are fairly rigid and resistant to changes, which on the one hand leads to legal certainty, but on the other hand leads to inflexible plans that are not appropriate for anticipating future changes. Something else that is important here are the fees which the municipality can levy when a developer takes an initiative that requires changing the plan or granting an exemption. If the municipality decides to change the plan in advance of new development it cannot recover the costs by fees. This can only be done when somebody requests a change. This practice is a disincentive for the municipality to change existing planning regimes. The municipality prefers to wait for another to take the initiative, as it can then get that other party to pay the transaction costs.

Changing *bestemmingsplannen* (or granting exemptions) is a money- and time-consuming activity. In Nijmegen there have been some experiments to make *bestemmingsplannen* for housing more flexible by making them broader, but the need and wish for (legal) certainty prevailed, and so the practice of making detailed customised plans, instead of bigger flexible plans to anticipate the future, was reinforced. Recently, the municipality has decided to consolidate the 600 plans into 20 bigger plans. The old, small and detailed plans have become an obstacle to anticipating developments. It is uncertain whether the city will succeed in doing this and break with the convention of making small postage plans to facilitate development initiatives.

## Agreement

The agreements – the intention and the development agreement – that had to be signed, took many years. The deliberations, together with the building drawings, started in 1994 and were finalised by contract in August 2000. The agreements were the result of two conditions. First, the land use plan had to be changed. As already mentioned, this gives a major resource to municipalities who can decide under which conditions, which can be spatial, procedural or financial, it wishes to cooperate. Other examples (in the city of Arnhem) of this practice can be found in Buitelaar *et al.* (2006). But this will be discussed in more detail in Chapter 8.

Secondly, because the developer was not able to acquire the land from the builders' merchant, the municipality acquired the plot. This made KDO even more dependent on the municipality. In addition, the developer needed to exchange land for public uses with building land. Therefore there was a high level of interdependence between the parties, and the developer was particularly dependent on the city of Nijmegen. This gave the municipality the advantage of being able to impose requirements on the developer to cover the transaction costs that were made by the city.

## Planning permission

It is difficult to assess the costs of the planning permission itself, because the actual costs that the municipality incurs for seeing the application through the various departments, need not be the same as the building fees it charges for doing so (building fees are different from the fees mentioned earlier that need to be paid for changing the *bestimmingsplan* or granting an exemption). Regular building permissions cost the municipality approximately 3200 Euros (at 2006 price level)[4] on average. The fee is, however, 1.45% of the total investment costs, which in this project means a total of 134 000 Euros of building fees. When the costs rise, the fee rises, while the costs of using the planning system do not rise at the same pace. It is plausible to assume that the costs of using this system for reviewing the plan of one house are not significantly higher than the costs for reviewing a plan of a hundred houses. The system is based on solidarity, which means that the bigger developments pay for the smaller, because covering the real costs of the smaller developments could mean higher fees than the building or investment costs. In 2006, the annual report of the building and housing department showed that it had more benefits from the building fees (3 962 461 Euros) than costs (3 488 804 Euros). These amounts include other permissions related to building, which also apply to the Marialaan case. Beside the costs of the building permission, some other permissions had to be applied for (and granted), such as permission for demolishing the existing structures on the site.

To recap, most transaction costs with regard to the user rights regime were made in the earlier and more informal stages of the development process. Much time and money was spent on land acquisition and deliberation between the developer and the municipality before the plan entered the formal *bestemmingsplan* and planning permission stages. The municipality was involved significantly from the early stages and therefore bore many transaction costs. It was, however, able to cream off some of the benefits from the developer to cover the transaction costs that the city of Nijmegen made during the process.

---

[4] This amount consists of 17 hours (building engineer) + 3 hours (review for conformance with the *bestemmingsplan*) + 21 hours (inspections), multiplied by 73 Euros per hour, makes 2993 Euros. Together with 100 Euros for the fire department and 100 Euros for the environmental department, the total amount comes at 3193 Euros (information provided by Kemperman and Alberts).

# References

Booth, P. (1996) *Controlling Development. Certainty and Discretion in Europe, the USA and Hong Kong.* UCL Press, London.

Booth, P. (2002a) From property rights to public control; the quest for public interest in the control of urban development. *Town Planning Review* **73**(2): 153–69.

Buitelaar, E., Mertens, H., Needham, B. & De Kam, G. (2006) *Sturend Vermogen en Woningbouw: Een Onderzoek naar het Vermogen van Gemeenten om te Sturen bij de Ontwikkeling van Woningbouwlocaties.* DGW/NETHUR, Den Haag/Utrecht.

De Kam, G. (1996) *Op Grond van Beleid. Locaties voor Sociale Woningbouw, Grondbeleid en Ruimtelijke Spreiding van Welstand in en rond Den Haag.* Nationale Woningraad, Almere.

Faludi, A. (2005) The Netherlands: a culture with a soft spot for planning. In: B. Sanyal (ed.), *Comparative Planning Cultures*, pp. 285–307. Routledge, New York.

Jacobs, H. M. (ed.) (1998) *Who Owns America?: Social Conflict Over Property Rights.* The University of Wisconsin Press, Madison WI.

Korthals Altes, W. K. & Groetelaers, D. A. (2000) De ntwikkeling van itbreidingslocaties: context en praktijk. *Achtergrondinformatie*, (1): 35–45.

Moroni, S. (2005) *Planning and the Rule of Law.* Vienna, AESOP conference.

Needham, D. B., Kruyt, B. & Koenders, P. (1993) *Urban Land and Property Markets in the Netherlands.* UCL Press, London.

Newman, P. & Thornley, A. (1996) *Urban Planning in Europe: International Competition, National Systems & Planning Projects.* Routledge, London/New York.

Nijland, H. G. M. (2005) Ontwikkelingen rond de apparaatskosten bij de bouwgrondproductie. *Achtergrondinformatie* (2): 43–52.

Overwater, P. S. A. (2002) *Naar een Sturend (Gemeentelijk) Grondbeleid. Wie de Grond Heeft, die Bouwt.* Kluwer, Alphen aan den Rijn.

Teijmant, I. (1988) Grondeigendom in ons cultuurpatroon. *Sociologische Gids* **35**(5): 302–19.

Van den Bergh, G. C. J. J. (1979) *Eigendom: Grepen uit de Geschiedenis van een Omstreden Begrip.* Kluwer, Deventer.

Van Hoek, B. (2004) Plankosten voor ruimtelijke ontwikkelingen. *SerVicE* **12**(1): 29–31.

Zweigert, K. & Kötz, H. (1987) *An Introduction to Comparative Law.* Clarendon Press, Oxford.

# 5

# Bristol: Planning in Uncertainty

In this chapter, the English case study is analysed. This is a housing site in the heart of the city of Bristol, called Wapping Wharf. Before going into the details of development process of Wapping Wharf, some key features of the English spatial planning and property rights regime are discussed. After the description of the development process, a transaction-cost analysis of the user rights regime will be made.

## English planning and property law

Booth (2002a, p. 154) argues that the way spatial planning is carried out in a country is intimately linked to the ideas about private property rights. When we compare the way the English think about property with the way the Dutch do, we get a better understanding of the differences between the spatial planning regimes in both countries. So first, a very brief overview of English land law will be given, after which the spatial planning regime, in particular development control, will be set out more extensively.

### Land law[1]

English law makes a distinction between personal and real property. Real property refers to immovable, and personal property to movable goods. Realty, as real property is also called, can be divided in corporeal hereditaments and incorporeal hereditaments. The first category

---

[1] This section is based on Haley (2004).

comprises inheritable things that can be physically possessed, like land and buildings. Incorporeal hereditaments are inheritable rights that cannot be possessed, like easements, profits and restrictive covenants.

Since the Norman conquest in 1066 and the introduction of feudalism, the Crown technically owns all the land in England. This means that an individual cannot own the land but can only own an estate in land. Starting with the sovereign at the top, a complex feudal pyramid of land estates and tenures was created, based on the concepts of *feudum* and *beneficium* (see also, Chapter 4). This is also called the doctrine of estates and the doctrine of tenures. The doctrine of tenure deals with the conditions on which land is held, whereas the doctrine of estates deals with the length of time for which land is held. Both have many subdivisions. The most important subdivision of estates is between freehold (which again can be subdivided in four categories) and leasehold (that is, less than freehold). The duration of a freehold is unlimited, while the duration of leasehold is fixed.

In 1925, property law in England was significantly changed by the Land and Property Act, among other acts, which aimed (among others things) at reducing the number of tenures and estates. Although this was achieved to a certain extent, the feudal origins of English land law are still clearly visible. Fragmentation of ownership and the high number of leasehold interests that can rest on the land, make land assembly a difficult, time-consuming and expensive process, since all must be acquired piecemeal. Failure to acquire all may frustrate the whole process (Williams & Wood, 1994). Moreover, in a study on ownership constraints for urban regeneration, in which 84 regeneration sites were analysed, the division of ownership rights was the most prevalent constraint (Adams *et al.*, 2002). The Bristol example shows some of these difficulties.

## Planning law[2]

Planning law adapts to land law, which makes it interesting to start with a brief comparison of land law in the Netherlands and England in order to understand the differences in planning law. We have to compare the feudal origins of the British property rights regime with the

---

[2] It must be noted that after the case study was carried out the law was changed by the adoption of the Planning and Compulsory Purchase Act 2004. In this chapter, the reform of the English planning system is not taken into account.

ideas of absolute ownership in the Netherlands, based on Roman law. In England, the feudal and common law tradition have led to a situation in which property rights have not been clearly codified and defined. The result has been that planning is associated with resolving *private* disputes over property rights. In some senses, notwithstanding the progression made since the Law of Property Acts 1921–5, property rights are still less clearly defined than, for example, in France (Booth, 2002a, p. 168) and in the Netherlands. Although the Town and Country Planning Act of 1947 tried to make a clearer distinction between the private and the public interest, by nationalising development rights, development control is still often used to resolve private disputes (Booth, 2002a). Cullingworth & Nadin (2002) say that internalising externalities is the basic feature of the English planning system, which is also characterised by the term 'land use management'(Nadin *et al.*, 1997). This seems to be more modest than the ambitions of the Dutch, who prefer a comprehensive and integrated approach.

With regard to the relationship between property rights and spatial planning, there is another major difference between the Netherlands and England. In the Netherlands, the law on property is more or less based on absolute ownership. A restriction by the state, for example, by designating a certain type of land use, is seen as an attenuation of the right to use property. The state is legitimised to do this. In England, there is no doctrine of *imperium*. The right to future development has been separated from the right to use, by the earlier mentioned nationalisation of development rights. Granting a planning permission in England is seen as giving the right to future development[3] (Booth, 2002b), which seems to go back to the concept of *beneficium*.

The differences in the relationship between property rights and spatial planning in the Netherlands and in England can also be seen when we delve more deeply into the development control systems of both. Generally, in England there is more emphasis on discretion and flexibility, while in the Netherlands (and most of the rest of continental Europe) there is more attention to the protection of property rights and legal certainty (Booth, 1996; Cullingworth & Nadin, 2002).

------

[3] Theoretically, I argue that there is no nationalisation of development rights. A right is a right when the owner of the right can exercise it. This is not the case with development rights, because the state can only grant them to the owner of the right to use and not exercise it itself. Therefore, from a theoretical perspective, planning conditions in England are, just like in other countries, an attenuation of the right to use property.

The Netherlands have a limited-imperative regime. This means that there is a limited and known number of conditions (Section 44, Woningwet, Housing Act) which a planning application must satisfy, while in England there are 'material considerations' (in or outside the development plan) that have to be taken into account *after* a planning application has been submitted (Sections 70 and 72, Town and Country Planning Act). Although this is not as open-ended as it might seem at first sight, due to policy guidelines and jurisprudence, it nevertheless gives local planning authorities a lot of flexibility.

In addition, the conditions in the Netherlands are imperative, which means that if the application meets the conditions, planning permission has to be granted to the applicant. There are no other conditions that can be raised if one wants to get planning permission (Van Buuren, *et al.*, 1999). In England 'almost all permissions are conditional' (Cullingworth & Nadin, 2002, p. 135), as granting planning permission is seen as the state giving the applicant a right to future development. The assumption is that if you give something that the other really wants, you are allowed to ask something in return, that is, impose conditions. In the Netherlands, conditions cannot be imposed on a planning permission. Planning permission is regarded as executing the decision made previously (e.g. in the land use plan) to restrict the right to develop/use land. The principle is: if the state wants to restrict someone's right to use land, it must make that explicit in advance.

Next to the 'planning conditions', England has the concept of 'planning obligations'. Dutch law does not allow obligations to be imposed with regard to land use within the WRO (see also, Overwater, 2002, p. 62), only prohibitions. The concept that is related to planning obligations is 'planning gain'. This means that the local authority grants permission only if the developer pays for related works, like infrastructure and open spaces. The agreement between the developer and the local authority is reached 'voluntarily'. This implies that the applicant cannot appeal against 'planning obligations', while he can appeal against 'planning conditions'[4].

---

[4]  It should be noted that Section 106B of the Town and Country Planning Act 1990 '[...] provides for a right of a appeal to the Secretary of State when a local planning authority fails to determine an application for the discharge or modification of a planning obligation within the prescribed period for so doing, or determines that a planning obligation shall continue to have effect without modification' (Moore, 2002, p. 365).

The basic principles of the British planning system, set out in the Town and Country Planning Act 1947 and retained in subsequent legislation, are development control, development plans and central government supervision (Newman & Thornley, 1996, p. 42; for detailed, but accessible, accounts of English planning law see Duxbury, 2002; Moore, 2002).

## Development plan

Since the early 1990s, the development plan, and hence a more plan-led approach, has gained importance after some decades of project-led development (Newman & Thornley, 1996, p. 42; Cullingworth & Nadin, 2002, p. 98).

'The project-led approach gave confused signals to landowners and developers seeking to establish the value of their assets, while those concerned with environmental quality questioned the accountability of regulatory decisions made on an ad hoc basis' (Healey *et al.*, 1995, p. 7).

In Section 54A of the Town and Country Planning Act 1990 (as amended by the Planning and Compensation Act 1991) the development plan became the primary consideration in decisions about planning permission.

In Britain, there are three types of development plans at the local level and they relate to the different tiers of local government (for an overview of the local government structure and associated development plans, see Cullingworth and Nadin, 2002, pp. 60–61 in combination with pp. 99–100). In Britain, a two-tier system was established in 1963 for London, in 1972 for Scotland and in 1973 for the rest of England and Wales. One tier is the county council, which makes the *structure plan*, and the other tier is the district council that makes the *local plan*. In 1986, the Thatcher government decided to streamline local government in London and some other metropolitan areas. In these areas we find the third type of development plan, namely the *unitary development plan*, which is mandatory for the metropolitan district councils, the London boroughs and some other authorities, most of which are urban. The unitary development plan has two parts, one akin to the structure plan and the other to the local plan. Although much of the two-tier system remains across Britain, between 1995 and

1997 a number of non-metropolitan unitary authorities were established. These unitary councils make a structure plan and a local plan. Bristol became one of these non-metropolitan unitary councils on 1 April 1996 (Bristol City Council, 1997).

A structure plan is actually not a 'plan', but a written statement and a key diagram with a general vision on development. It has a 15-year horizon. The local plans have a time horizon of approximately 10 years. They must be in general conformity with the structure plan and national and regional guidance. Before adoption, plans are subject to extensive publicity, consultation and a period for formal objection (European Commission, 2000, p. 23).

Local plans are mandatory (since 1992) and area-wide (that is, covering the whole district or administrative area of a city). The decision on development control must accord with the development plan unless material considerations indicate otherwise (Section 54A, Town and Country Planning Act 1990). If an applicant wants to submit an application that is in conflict with the development plan, he 'would need to produce convincing reasons to demonstrate why the plan should not prevail' (Planning Policy Guidance 1).

After the case study was carried out (and after Wapping Wharf had been developed), the system for the development plan in England changed as a result of the Planning and Compulsory Purchase Act 2004. Whilst national planning guidance remains largely unchanged, with the introduction of Planning Policy Statements to replace Planning Policy Guidance notes, arrangements in the lower tiers of government are very different. Regional spatial strategies are required to be produced at a regional level and structure plans have been abolished, but it is at the local level that the main changes will occur. The new system has been designed to 'streamline the local planning process and promote a proactive, positive approach to managing development' (Planning Policy Statement 12). The development plan will consist of a regional spatial strategy and development plan documents, the latter setting the local development framework (LDF). Various plans and policies will be included in the LDF, including, for example, a core strategy, a statement of community involvement, action area plans, a proposals map and other supplementary planning documents. The latter might be most useful in development control, since they may include design guidance or master plans for a particular site. The new act retains the spirit of Section 54A (Town and Country Planning Act, 1990) in that the development plan remains the essential framework for development control decisions in a plan-led system (Section 38(6), Planning and Compulsory Purchase Act, 2004).

**Development control**

Central to development control is the definition of development. In Section 55 of the Town and Country Planning Act 1990 development means 'the carrying out of building, engineering, mining or other operations in, on, over or under land, or the making of any material change in the use of any buildings or other land.' For carrying out development a planning permission is required[5]. A planning application must consist of a number of documents, namely an application form, a number of plans with varying levels of detail, a fee, and in some cases an environmental impact statement. In addition, as theoretically anyone can apply for planning permission, '[...] an applicant for planning permission shall give requisite notice of the application to any person (other than the applicant) who on the prescribed date is an owner of the land to which the application relates, or a tenant [...]' (Section 65 of the Town and Country Planning Act 1990). Development control has been separated from controls on building, pollution and transport.

As has been said before, the local development plan (and its replacement under the new act) is the primary consideration in the control of development. The local planning authority has to also take account of other material considerations, which include op received from publicity and consultation, environmental impact assessment, site characteristics, design and layout, access and parking arrangements. All the material considerations must be relevant to planning. The courts have come forward with an open-ended definition: 'any consideration which relates to the use and development of land is capable of being a planning consideration' (Moore, 2002). This can include social and financial factors as well.

Sometimes, certain goals in planning cannot be achieved by imposing planning conditions. Then, *planning obligations* may provide a solution. With the adoption of the Planning and Compensation Act in 1991, a new Section 106 (and 106A and 106B) was inserted in the Town and Country Planning Act 1990. The power to enter into a planning agreement was then replaced by the power to enter into a planning

---

[5] There are (minor) developments that are not subject to planning permission: the permitted developments. The Town and Country Planning (General Permitted Development) Order 1995 enumerates 33 classes of development that do not need approval from the local planning authority or the Secretary of State.

obligation (Moore, 2002, p. 355; for more details about the development of planning obligations, see also pp. 355–62 and Duxbury, 2002, pp. 325–31), which does not necessarily have to be agreed upon in a planning agreement. This law enables any person with an interest in land in the area of the local planning authority to enter into a planning obligation, which might be either given as a *unilateral undertaking* from the applicant or agreed by the local planning authority. These obligations run with the land. The obligations can be both restrictive as well as positive. Section 106 says that an obligation may restrict the development or use in some specified way; require specified operations to be carried out in, on, under or over land; require the land to be used in some specified way; or require a sum or sums to be paid to the authority on a specified date or dates or periodically. There is a specific requirement that the payments have to relate to the land itself or the development that is carried out (Moore, 2002, p. 363). Although planning conditions are often an appropriate means to achieve certain objectives, local planning authorities often prefer to negotiate an obligation (Healey *et al.*, 1995, p. 75). One reason planning officers give for this choice is the expectation that obligations are less likely to be broken than imposed conditions.

**The role of central government**

Central government plays an important role in British land use planning. The roles of the central government in development control are multiple (Newman & Thornley, 1996, p. 42). First, it makes legislation and issues national planning policy guidances (PPGs), (these are general rather than location-specific, and are now being systematically replaced by Planning Policy Statements (PPSs)), regional planning guidances (RPGs) and minerals planning guidances (MPGs)[6]. This has been done (since 2002) by the Office of the Deputy of the Prime Minister (ODPM), and before that by the Department for Transport, Local Government and the Regions (DTLR) (Cullingworth & Nadin, 2002, p. 45), and previously by the Department of the Environment (DoE)[7]. The PPGs are important considerations in development control

---

[6] Central government also publishes circulars that are primarily used to explain the legislation. In recent years, the content of many circulars has been replaced by PPGs (and PPSs).

[7] And the name changed once again; at the moment of writing the ODPM was changed into Department for Communities and Local Government (DCLG).

decisions because central government is the level where applicants can appeal against development control decisions.

This is the second role of central government in development control. The Secretaries of State (ministers responsible for planning) have extensive formal powers. An unsuccessful planning applicant can (and this often done, see chart on p. 137 of Cullingworth & Nadin, 2002) go to an appeal to the Secretary of State (Cullingworth & Nadin, 2002, pp. 136–139). This type of appeal is possible only on policy grounds, for points of law the applicant must go to court (European Commission, 2000). Appeals to the Secretary of State are allowed when planning permission is refused, against planning conditions, when the local planning authority has failed to make a decision within the prescribed period, and on enforcement notices. There is no right of appeal from third parties. Almost all appeals are dealt with by the Planning Inspectorate (executive agency of the ODPM). Matters of major importance (approximately 1% of all the appeals) are dealt with by the Secretary of State (actually the senior civil servants in the department, but in reality often taken on political grounds, for example, decisions on new or expanded airports). The Secretary of State and the inspectors are allowed to reverse (both granting and refusing) the decision by the local authority, and add, delete or modify conditions.

Planning applications can also be called-in[8] by the Secretary of State. This can be done when the development is more than 150 houses or 10,000 m$^2$ of retail floorspace, when the land is owned by the local planning authority or if the development because of its scale or location would significantly prejudice the implementation of the development plan (European Commission, 2000, p. 79). Therefore, planning in England is more centralised than in the Netherlands and the US.

## Wapping Wharf

Wapping Wharf is part of an area in Bristol called Harbourside, which covers 27 hectares of former dock and industrial land in the centre of the city. For a long time hardly any regeneration took place in

---

[8] Section 77 of the Town and Country Planning Act 1990 provides the Secretary of State with the power to call in applications for his own determination instead of the local planning authority. This power is seldom used, only for some matters of more than local importance.

Harbourside until, in 1989, Lloyds TSB Bank built its headquarters on the north side of the dock after buying land from Imperial Tobacco and demolishing huge, unused, bonded warehouses. Bristol City Council, in granting permission, thought that this would act as a catalyst for further regeneration (Bristol City Council, 1998). At least it prompted a shift in planning policy from passive to active involvement of the local authority. The local authority started to cooperate with the landowners, developers and central government. Since the early 1990s, large amounts of money have been secured for the redevelopment of Harbourside.

Wapping Wharf was the first major housing scheme in Harbourside (Bristol City Council, 1998), although the first dockside housing scheme was at Baltic Wharf, just to the west. Until 1828 Wapping Wharf was an undeveloped greenfield site. Since 1886 the site had been used as railway sidings and was used as such until 1998. In the last years before development, it was also used as a car park.

The city council, the principal land owners (British Gas, British Railways, JT Group and Lloyds TSB) and the Bristol Chamber of Commerce and Initiative, united in 1993 as the Harbourside Sponsors Group. This group was set up to start a regeneration of Harbourside that was to be commercially viable and in line with the objectives of the different participants in the group.

The Harbourside Sponsors Group appointed a development facilitator, Drivers Jonas, (property consultants) to facilitate the process of preparing a development framework for the whole of Harbourside. To create the development framework three architects (Bruges Tozer, Alec French and Ferguson Mann), together called the Concept Planning Group (CPG), were appointed. In March 1994, the development framework was approved by the council's Planning and Development Committee and agreed by all sponsors in the 'Harbourside Accord'. In the development framework, Wapping Wharf was indicated (see Figure 5.1).

On behalf of the CPG, Bruges Tozer gave special attention to Spike Island, the area south of Floating Harbour (the canal that flows through the Harbourside area), and Wapping Wharf. The other two architects focused on Canon's Marsh, north of Floating Harbour.

The approval of the development framework led to the preparation and adoption, after a period of public consultation, of the Bristol Harbourside Planning Brief in June 1995. In this planning brief, Wapping Wharf was earmarked for residential development of approximately 140 units in the Bristol Harbourside Development Project Planning Brief. The Harbourside planning brief of the LPA in 1995

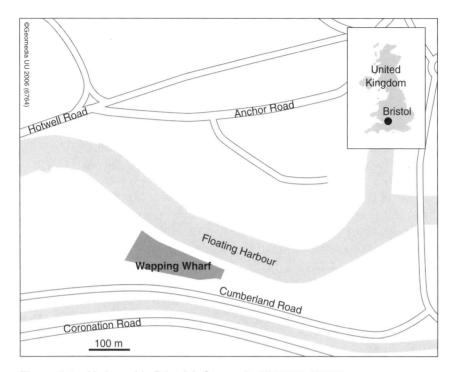

**Figure 5.1**   Harbourside Bristol © Geomedia UU 2006 (6764).

followed the development framework. The Royal Town Planning Institute (Allinson & Askew, 1996, p. 76) defines a development or planning brief as 'A summary statement of the author's policy position on development matters relating to a site and/or premises'. It is a site-specific, non-statutory policy document that must not be seen as the substitute for a statutory plan, but as a more detailed elaboration complementary to the local plan.

The 1995 planning brief formed a supplementary guidance to the local plan that was, at the moment of adoption of the planning brief, in the public inquiry stage. The local plan was adopted in December 1997. This Bristol Local Plan had been adopted after a process of over five years of consultations, public inquiries and modifications (Bristol City Council, 1997, p. 14)[9] and was the first area-wide plan for the city of Bristol in twenty years.

---

[9]  It has been prepared under the rules of the Town and Country Planning Act 1990 and PPG 12. There are few statutory phases in the process of the local plan. This is found to be inappropriate due to the variations in planning issues and the degree of support to plan proposals (see PPG 12).

In the local plan, Harbourside is proposed as a 'major regeneration area' of the city centre. The content of the proposal is: 'development for a new office quarter, major leisure/tourist facilities and ancillary shopping for housing, in a mixed use form' (Bristol City Council, 1997, p. 225). There is also room reserved in the plans for new housing, particularly in Wapping Wharf (and Canon's Marsh). Wapping Wharf is seen as an 'attractive waterside "urban village"' (Ibid, p. 226).

In July 1998, a new planning brief (called Bristol Harbourside Regeneration Planning Brief) was approved by the Planning, Transport and Development Committee of the Bristol City Council. This planning brief gave supplementary guidance to the local plan of December 1997 and was directed to implementation of the regeneration policy. Wapping Wharf was still earmarked as a housing site.

The land in the whole Harbourside was in several ownerships (see above). The City Council, British Railways Board (which owned most of the land at Spike Island), and British Gas (which owned some of the land at Canon's Marsh) poded their land for one integrated development, selling it off to various parties around 1996. After the adoption of the development framework (in 1994) and the planning brief (in 1995), Bruges Tozer together with Alec French (as part of the CPG) approached Beaufort (which was a subsidiary of the Barclay group; at the time of the research their name had changed to Crosby Special Projects) as a possible developer. Bruges Tozer thought Beaufort, in combination with itself as member of the Concept Planning Group, would be most likely to receive a planning permission. Beaufort was relatively new to Bristol; it had only done greenfield developments in the area until then, but had much experience with up-market redevelopment in London, Birmingham and other provincial regions (Lambert & Boddy, 2002).[10] Bruges Tozer drafted various alternatives. With a rough sketch, Beaufort (and Bruges Tozer) went into the bidding process for the land in 1996. Their bid did not win, because Beaufort did not put enough money in it. There was another developer with whom the city council went along, but after a while the city council decided that the scheme was not good enough and that the developer did not have enough credibility. So it went out for a

---

[10] Lambert & Boddy (2002) note that Beaufort, and many other big national developers, undertake these city centre redevelopment projects to diversify their portfolio, where their traditional emphasis was on greenfield land and suburban housing. This is mainly driven by the government's brownfield land target.

competition again a year later in 1997. This time Beaufort did win with more or less the same scheme, but more money. This was then 'approved' by the Property and Finance department of the City Council and Beaufort bought the land in September 1997 from British Rail Property.

Beaufort then entered the stage of seeking planning permission. Before it submitted the application, it held several meetings with the residents and the planning officers. Two meetings were held (in October 1997) with the residents and two with the planning officers (in September and October 1997). There was also a preliminary investigation of the level of soil contamination, which showed that there was little contamination, for the site had only been used as a transfer point of coals from the ships to the train.

In October 1997, a preliminary application was submitted to the local planning authority. Between this application and the application for full planning permission (in January 1998) there was one meeting with the residents (in October 1997) and one with the planning officers (in November 1997). The planning officers were reluctant to get into a discussion about the scheme. This is a general problem, for local planning authorities are short-staffed related to the number of planning applications they have to deal with (see also Allinson & Askew, 1996).

After the submission for the full planning permission there was one meeting (in January 1998) with the residents and three with the planning officers (in April, July and August 1998). There were also discussions about conditions and a draft Section 106 agreement. The officers were keen to grant planning permission, so they recommended it for approval.

There was concerted opposition to the scheme. The people who live and lived on Cumberland Road, the road adjacent to the site (see Figure 5.1) are very articulate (possibly, according to Nigel Honer, because many work in media). The residents particularly opposed the number of storeys and the obscuring effect they would have on the waterside. After this meeting, changes were made to the proposal and more detail was added to it. According to Bruges Tozer, there was a constant pressure on them as architects from two sides: the opposition against the number of storeys by the residents on the one hand, and on the other hand the requirement of the developer to keep the number of dwellings as high as possible to increase the profits. The developer kept pressure on Bruges Tozer to disguise the height of the buildings by manipulating the drawings. All the alterations to the scheme were fairly cosmetic and the residents accused Beaufort/Bruges Tozer on this point. The period between the preliminary and full planning application was short. The developer was 'massively overconfident' (to quote Nigel Honer again) that they were providing the best scheme for the residents on Cumberland Road. There was not enough time to work on further details of the scheme in order to give it a more friendly appearance, and the application as submitted showed an image of very sharp cut blocks generated by the computer. The developer was more interested in the economics of the scheme (maximising the benefits and minimising the costs) than its design.

As a result of the consultations, three major amendments were made to the scheme: one between the preliminary application and the full application, and two after the full application. Most amendments had to do with the height of the buildings and some with off-site works.

In December 1998 the Planning Committee proposed rejection of the planning permission after a big lobby by the residents, mainly those living at the Cumberland Road. Finally both planning and building regulations permission were rejected. At the same time as the application for full planning permission (and building regulations), an application was submitted for the modification of the existing car park to provide access to the site. This permission was granted in June 1998. Beaufort went to an appeal against the rejection of the scheme; although it withdrew from this later. The threat of an appeal had probably been used to keep the pressure on the local planning authority to grant the permission.

At the same time, different architects were employed (Feilden Clegg) to make a new plan in a more participatory way. This was done to show the people that Beaufort wanted to make a new start that was not purely cosmetic. Beaufort employed an independent chairman (Jeff Bishop) to chair four meetings (in January, February, March and April 1999) with all interest groups involved, called 'Reaching agreement on Wapping Wharf'. This public consultation is probably the main reason why this scheme was approved and granted planning permission[11].

---

[11] Nigel Honer thinks that the people are now worse off because of the very modern (un-British) architecture. That was the reason why the building proved to be difficult to sell. He does not think that this scheme has contributed to making that part of Bristol a better urban space (see also the book by Tony Aldous called *Bristol's Twentieth Century Buildings*). The developer may not have maximised profits because the scheme was difficult to sell and because of the long process.

With this public consultation there were few or no political reasons left for refusing the permission. However, it did not mean that there were no objections[12].

In May 1999 Beaufort, together with British Rail Property submitted a full planning application (together with a fee cheque enclosed of £ 9,500, and an environmental assessment[13]). It also submitted an application (for a Conservation Area Consent) to demolish a building and a brick wall in order to let the development proceed[14]. After the application was submitted, three sets of amendments were made (in July, August and October). Only the third set, because of the nature and scale of the changes, led to new public consultation. This led to complaints from the residents of nearby dwellings. One of the residents even called the process chosen by the local planning authority an 'underhand way'.

In October 1999 the Planning, Transport and Development (Central) Area Sub-Committee assembled and recommended that the permission (also the Conservation Area Consent) should be granted, subject to conditions and a Section 106 agreement, and this was finalised in November 1999. Permission was granted for the erection of five buildings varying in height between three and six storeys, comprising nine dwellings, 105 apartments and a cafe. In addition 113 car parking spaces needed to be provided and landscape and quayside works had to be carried out. The main elements of the planning permission and the Section 106 agreement are to be found in Box 1.

There were 33 planning conditions attached to the planning permission. All these conditions had to be 'discharged in writing' by the local planning authority to the developer once they had been implemented. The developer had to show that he has complied with the conditions satisfactorily. At the moment of the empirical research (Spring 2004), not all of the conditions had been discharged such as, for example, Condition 5 ii which relates to a cycle-footpath connection

---

[12] A petition was handed in to the committee to protest against the development on Wapping Wharf because it would deprive 'the whole community' of a much valued inner city view. It was signed by 1375 signatories! Another 15 letters of objection were sent.

[13] The Environmental Assessment has been criticised heavily by the Environmental Health Department, especially the noise assessment (derived from correspondence between the city of Bristol and the developer).

[14] More precisely, this consent comprised the demolition of a single storey building to the east of the existing toilet block and demolition of the northern boundary wall to the SS Great Britain car park.

**Box 1**    The content of the planning permission and Section 106 agreement at Wapping Wharf

**Planning permission**

The planning permission, which was granted 16 November 1999, allowed the building of 114 houses, 113 parking spaces and a cafe under certain conditions. Many conditions are both procedural and substantive. These conditions prescribe which activities should be carried out by the developer and the procedural requirements, such as 50 percent occupation of the dwellings, attached to that. The most important conditions are (not literally quoted):

- no dwelling shall be occupied until the road and footpath that give access to the site are constructed according to the approved plan;
- no more than 50% of the dwellings shall be occupied until the quayside works are carried out as approved;
- no more than 50% of the dwellings shall be occupied until an off-site cycle and footpath (see also Section 106 agreement) is constructed;
- no more than 50% of the dwellings shall be occupied until further details about the car parking are submitted and approved by the local planning authority;
- detailed drawings at a large scale (of a list of elements given in the decision notice) shall be submitted and approved before any work is commenced on the relevant part of the development;
- samples of the materials used (of a list of elements given in the decision notice) shall be submitted and approved before any work is commenced on the relevant part of the development;
- no more than 50% of the dwellings shall be occupied until details of a scheme of external lighting and seating has been submitted;
- before works are carried out, measures to minimise dust and noise shall be submitted;
- before any residential accommodation is occupied the car parking and garaging areas need to be completed;
- no more than 50% of the dwellings shall be occupied until details of the amenity/play areas have been submitted;
- an archaeological watching brief shall be conducted during all ground work operations to record any archaeological features and deposits that may be encountered. This work shall be undertaken by an archaeologist to be approved by the local planning authority (but paid by the developer);

---

**Box 1** (*Continued*)

**Section 106 agreement**

- the soft landscaping shall be carried out no later than the first planting season;
- no more than 50% of the dwellings shall be occupied until the hard landscaping works are completed.

Most important planning obligations (literally quoted):

- 'Off site junction improvements to the Gas Ferry Road/Cumberland Road Junction subject to detailed design and technical approval by the City Council of the Off Site Landscape Works shown on Drawing No 904/109 attached to this Agreement'.
- 'The Developer shall construct a footpath/cycleway link on the Yellow Land in accordance with details to be agreed with the Council in order to provide a link under the Cumberland Road to the Chocolate Path'.

---

along the railway track, which is off-site. But the railway company (which was the owner of that piece of land) did not allow the developer to carry out the works. To resolve the issue the local planning authority has agreed with the railway company that the local planning authority can develop the path, and they have been given right of access for one pound and the developer pays the local planning authority for these works . Although the conditions specified that no more than 50 % of the new dwellings could be occupied before that time, the local planning authority knew what was going on and wanted to solve the problem, instead of enforcing the condition.

It might also happen that while executing a planning permission, one or more conditions prove to be unnecessary or unreasonable. Then, the applicant must apply for a change or deletion of the condition (this is an application under the provisions of Section 73 of the Town and Country Planning Act 1990). At Wapping Wharf two conditions, relating to noise mitigation measures, were deleted because they were found to be excessive measures for the problem at hand. To support the application, a consultant was employed to carryout a noise assessment and write a report about it. The buildings were finished in

November 2001, but discharging all the conditions took some more years. The same counts for the sale of all the apartments. At the moment of the empirical research, there were still two apartments unsold.

## Transaction-cost analysis of Wapping Wharf

In this section, the transaction costs associated with the user rights regime are of central concern. In Table 5.1, an overview of the important transaction costs related to the creation and use of the user rights regime at Wapping Wharf is given. In the following subsections these elements are elaborated.

### Land exchange

There were several moments in the development process where land acquisition, or an attempt to acquire land, played an important role. The first moment was when Beaufort acquired the land for development. Beaufort bought the land from British Rail Property in 1997 after a fairly long (and transaction-cost consuming) bidding procedure. First, in 1996, it did not bid enough money to acquire the site, but in 1997 when the joint land owners of Harbourside issued a new bidding procedure, Beaufort offered enough to buy the land from the railway company. Beaufort acquires land only for development and does not have a land bank. Therefore Beaufort has a close network of agents and all sorts of other contacts that identify land for them. This network is crucial for their strategy to buy land for development that can be 'turned around' quickly.

Usually when Beaufort acquires land it takes some time (3 to 4 weeks) for the solicitors to sort out what it is specifically that it buys. Because of previous developments, certain pieces of a site may be left unused (for example, because of the shape), and these are difficult to sell. These pieces may just remain there 'unowned' and later, when a site is sold again, it may happen that nobody knows who the landowner is. This was the case with a small piece of land just off site that was needed for the required cycle/footpath along the railway track. Almost all the land was owned by British Rail Property, except for one piece underneath a bridge (junction with the Cumberland Road, see Figure 5.1). Because of this, the condition

**Table 5.1** Transaction costs at Wapping Wharf

| Activities | Indication of the amount | Borne by |
|---|---|---|
| **1. Land exchange** | | |
| Acquisition of the site by Beaufort | Two bidding procedures in 1996 and 1997, plus employing agents and solicitors | Mainly the **developer** (employing agents and solicitors) and to a lesser extent the joint land owners (so also **Bristol City Council**) who issued the bidding procedure |
| Attempt by Bristol City Council to acquire land for an electronic bus | Has taken a long time (years), but neither party could agree on the price | **Bristol City Council** |
| Sale of the apartments | | **Developer** |
| **2. Land use or zoning plan** | | |
| Planning brief 1995 | few months | *Bristol City Council* |
| Making the local plan 1997 (vision on the city until 2001) | 1992–1997, five years and, to a much lesser extent, | mainly the **Bristol City Council** <br><br> the **developer** (lobby work) |
| Planning brief 1998 | few months | **Bristol City Council** |
| **3. Agreement** | | |
| Negotiation around the Section 106 agreement | The period between the submission of the planning application and granting the planning permission: seven months | Mainly by the **developer** and to a lesser extent the **Bristol City Council** |
| **4. Planning permission** | | |
| Preparation planning application (and an Environmental Assessment) | Since the land acquisition in 1997 until the application in May 1999 (rejected once), plus a fee of £9500 | Mainly the **developer** |
| Planning permission (negotiation and modifications proposal) | Seven months after application | Both **the developer** and the **Bristol City Council** |
| Discharging conditions (and realising planning obligations) | Some quickly, others took (and are taking) years | Mainly the **developer** who has to comply with the conditions satisfactorily and, to a lesser extent, the **Bristol City Council** that has to discharge the conditions by writing |
| Building regulation approval[a] | | Both **the developer** and **Bristol City Council** |

[a] A building regulation approval is given by a different set of people, called Building Inspectors, who work separately from the planners. It concerns details of the buildings to make sure that they comply with the building regulations – mainly to do with health and safety, fire, and so on in accordance with a set of (very complex) standards.

relating to the foot and cycle path has not yet been discharged (see above).

A particular piece of land can have an enormous history attached to it. Solicitors have to sort out whether there is a chance that an owner or someone with a legitimate interest might show up and claim a certain right over that land. Another project of Beaufort in Bristol is Redland. After that site had been developed, the neighbours (adjoining owners) came along to say that there was a right of access at the back of the buildings. They provided evidence for this claim by showing a document from the Land Registry. Beaufort was lucky not to have built on that particular part, so it was not too difficult to provide that access. But it shows that even though solicitors carry out extensive investigations, it does not mean that everything is completely clear. The uncertainty caused by unclear registration of land can lead to significant transaction costs.

Another moment in the development process of Wapping Wharf when there was an attempt to acquire land, was when the local planning authority wanted to buy land from the railway company for the operation of the Bristol Electric Bus (BER). This is a flywheel powered bus that is supposed to run up and down the waterside between Wapping Wharf and the Museum of Bristol (see Figure 6.1). In the end it proved to be impossible to make the bus work. The Bristol City Council had tried to buy the land for the BER, but did not succeed. Compulsory purchase has not been used because it is very complex and takes a long time. In Bristol, compulsory purchase has recently only been applied to the extension of the main shopping centre in the middle of the city. If the local authority cannot acquire the land amicably it usually retreats or tries to find different solutions to achieve its purposes. One might be 'a public right of way', which is an easement on a piece of land.

More generally, because there is no legally binding land use plan, different ways have to be sought by developers (and other applicants) to increase their certainty about what is allowed to happen on a particular piece of land in the future. Oxley (2004, p. 212) says:

'[...] a lack of clarity in the planning system, a large degree of discretionary power by the planning authorities and much room for negotiation may be seen to increase uncertainty and impose additional costs on development.'

Before a developer, or any other person who wants to develop land, buys a plot, he wants to be fairly sure that after buying that land he can develop it. As the local plan, or informal documents like planning briefs, are not legally binding and the guidance is often very general and open to interpretation (especially compared to the *bestemmings-plan*), not much certainty is provided in advance. In the Netherlands, a land use plan is legally binding and if an application fits within the plan it has to be granted. If it does not, an exemption from or a revision of the plan is needed. In England, a developer might either buy the land, not knowing whether he will be able to build on it later, or try to get planning permission before he buys it. Because anyone can apply for a planning permission – not only the owner of a plot – developers often try to get planning permission before they buy the land for development. Obviously, the permission can only be used if they have the land.

Land can be acquired in various ways. This can be either in a one-to-one negotiation, a bidding procedure against other developers, or an auction. In case of an auction, the sale date is fixed and therefore there is little time to try to acquire planning permission. It might also happen that if planning permission has been granted to a developer, the initial landowner may decide not to sell the land because the permission granted may have given the land a great development potential, from which the landowner wants to benefit. Therefore, especially for the bigger sites, a developer might decide to take out an option on the land in order to secure his right to buy it until he has been able to acquire the permission.

## Land use or zoning plan

The Bristol Local Plan of 1997 is the primary consideration for determining planning applications. This plan covers the whole city. The plan-making process took over five years from the first consultations till the adoption of the plan in December 1997.

The planning briefs of 1995 and 1998 are not statutory documents, but are nevertheless important documents for further delineation of the spatial policy of the city council, and therewith provide some certainty for potential developers. They are supplementary (and more detailed) guidance to the Bristol Local Plan.

## Agreement

Unlike the agreements in the Dutch case, which were agreements under private law, the Section 106 agreement is an agreement under public law, namely Section 106 of the Town and Country Planning Act of 1990. The Section 106 agreement is attached to the planning permission. In this particular case the planning permission was subject to the Section 106 agreement. After the planning application has been submitted, not only the planning permission is discussed but also the content of the Section 106 agreement. In this case, the local planning authority wanted the developer to carry out some off-site works for the benefit of the local community.

A transaction-cost issue that is important for the developer, is the lack of knowledge in advance of the content of the planning obligations. There is usually uncertainty about which obligations the local planning authority requires. Although 89% of local planning authorities have an affordable housing policy written down in the local plan, a common complaint among developers is that policy changes a lot, which leads to an inconsistent message (Crook *et al.*, 2002, pp. 17–18). This may lead to more negotiations and hence to higher transaction costs.

## Planning permission

Altogether, the whole planning permission process has taken a relatively long time as the permission was initially rejected. One could say that the main reason for the rejection, and therewith the rise in transaction costs, was the attitude of Beaufort towards involvement of the public. In addition, 'Bristol has more than its fair share of influential conservation groups' (from an interview with Ian Thomas). Local knowledge and a good relationship with both planning officers and the community are important and can help to keep transaction costs down. On the other hand, initial investments are needed to build this knowledge and these networks.

Another transaction-cost raising factor that was mentioned (in an interview with Nigel Honer) is the local guidance. The local guidance is usually non-quantified (the number of storeys, densities or number of dwellings are not specified) and is written in general words, without much detail and without any maps and drawings. The Lloyds building (the circle- and crescent-shaped building on the north side of Floating Harbour), which is five storeys high, was taken as the point of reference for the rest of Harbourside. But five storeys of an office building equate to seven storeys of a residential building. The lack of illustrations and maps, more generally the lack of precision in the terms used, is regarded as the reason that the content of the local guidance was not clear.

The preparation of the application had already started before the land acquisition in September 1997, and it took until May 1999 before the planning permission was finally granted. Between the rejection of the first scheme and the application for the scheme that was approved, Beaufort set up an interactive plan-making process. This improved the chances of Beaufort getting planning permission the second time.

After the permission has been granted, there is still some uncertainty left. Almost every permission is conditional. These conditions have to be discharged in writing by the local planning authority. So after the permission has been granted there is still some discretionary power for the local authorities to control the content of the proposed development. Planning conditions are also often used to postpone some decisions, until the developer provides more details.

The income that local authorities get from central government has been made dependent (among other things) on the speed of processing planning applications. The higher the number of planning decisions made within either eight or thirteen weeks, the higher the grants (that is, Planning Delivery Grants) the local authority receives. Therefore, local planning authorities try to handle the applications quickly. This speeding up of the planning application procedure should speed up the whole process. But in practice, because many applications are too complex to be decided upon within eight weeks, they are either refused or conditions are imposed, covering for instance design, to be sorted out in a later stage. The rule also limits negotiations during the passage of a planning application, since planning officers do not have time to ask for better designs, and so forth. More attention to the working of the Planning Delivery Grants will be paid in Chapter 8.

In the case of Wapping Wharf, after the planning permission had been given, there was a lot of correspondence on the imposed conditions and how to get them discharged. Some issues resulted in extensive negotiation. For instance, the street lighting and the fence between the project and the existing housing (at Cumberland Road) has led to discussion and correspondence. This might also be an important reason why Beaufort had to employ many different agents and consultants. If they wanted to change a certain type of material, they employed an external consultant who is an expert in that particular field to deliver the necessary expertise and to persuade the local planning authority of the necessity.

Another issue that is interesting from the perspective of transaction costs is the wording of the conditions. Many conditions are broadly written, which might cause contention between the applicant and the local planning authority. This seems to have improved recently (interview Mike Devereux). In the case of the Wapping Wharf two conditions have not yet been discharged. A mistake that the local planning authority made was that the conditions and the Section 106 agreement were not consistent; the wording is not exactly the same. One condition that has not yet been discharged is the cycle- and footpath condition, because no one could find who owned the land (under the Cumberland Road). This emphasises the importance of clarity of planning conditions and Section 106 agreements.

Although the city of Bristol was involved from the very beginning, it was not as closely involved in the preparatory work of the developer as the city of Nijmegen was in the development. Its involvement was greatest during the review of the planning application and the negotiations about the Section 106 agreement, and afterwards in inspecting the site and discharging the conditions. Clarity and certainty, and sometimes the lack thereof, seem to be key words in the way the development process of Wapping Wharf proceeded. Bristol's local plan provides only limited guidance to developers but, on the other hand, also gives a lot of flexibility. I had assumed that once a planning permission had been granted, the developer would know exactly what to do. But there were still some, although slightly smaller, decisions to be made on design and material issues. The way the City of Houston deals with applications for development is the opposite to these discretionary practices.

# References

Adams, D., Disberry, A., Hutchison, N. & Munjoma, T. (2002) Land policy and urban renaissance: the impact of ownership constraints in four British cities. *Planning Theory and Practice* 3(2): 195–217.

Allinson, J. & Askew, J. (1996) Planning gain. In: C. Greed (ed.), *Implementing Town Planning: The Role of Town Planning in the Development Process*, pp. 62–72. Longman, London.

Booth, P. (1996) *Controlling Development. Certainty and Discretion in Europe, the USA and Hong Kong*. UCL Press, London.

Booth, P. (2002a) From property rights to public control; the quest for public interest in the control of urban development. *Town Planning Review* 73(2): 153–69.

Booth, P. (2002b) Nationalising development rights: the feudal origins of the British planning system. *Environment and Planning B* **29**: 129–39.

Bristol City Council (1997) Bristol Local Plan.

Bristol City Council (1998) Bristol Harbourside Regeneration Planning Brief.

Crook, T., Currie, J., Jackson, A., Monk, S., Rowley, S., Smith, K. & Whitehead, C. (2002) *Planning Gain and Affordable Housing: Make It Count*. University of Cambridge, Cambridge.

Cullingworth, B. & Nadin, V. (2002) *Town & Country Planning in the UK*, 13th edn. Routledge, London.

Duxbury, R. M. C. (2002) *Planning Law and Procedure*. LexisNexis Butterworths Tolley, London.

European Commission (2000) *The EU Compendium of Spatial Planning Systems and Policies: United Kingdom*. Office for Official Publications of the European Communities, Luxembourg.

Haley, M. (2004) *Land Law*. Sweet & Maxwell, London.

Healey, P., Purdue, M. & Ennis, F. (1995) *Negotiating Development: Rationales and Practice for Development Obligations and Planning Gain*. E & FN SPON, London.

Lambert, C. & Boddy, M. (2002) *Transforming the City: Post-Recession Gentrification and Re-urbanisation. Paper Presented to the 2002 AESOP Congress*. Volos, Greece, 10–13 July.

Moore, V. (2002) *A Practical Approach to Planning Law*. Oxford University Press, Oxford.

Nadin, V., Hawkes, P., Cooper, S., Shaw, D. & Westlake, T. (1997) *The EU Compendium of Spatial Planning Systems, Regional Development Studies 28*. European Commission, Brussels.

Newman, P. & Thornley, A. (1996) *Urban Planning in Europe: International Competition, National Systems & Planning Projects*. Routledge, London/New York.

Overwater, P. S. A. (2002) *Naar een Sturend (Gemeentelijk) Grondbeleid. Wie de Grond Heeft, die Bouwt*. Kluwer, Alphen aan den Rijn.

Oxley, M. (2004) *Economics, Planning And Housing*. Palgrave Macmillan, Basingstoke/New York.

Van Buuren, P. P. J., Backes, C. W. & De Gier, A. A. J. (1999) *Hoofdlijnen Ruimtelijk Bestuursrecht. Bestuursrecht – Theorie en Praktijk*. Kluwer, Deventer.

Williams, R. H. & Wood, B. (1994) *Urban Land and Property Markets in the UK*. UCL Press, London.

# 6

# Houston: Planning in the City That Does Not Plan?

This chapter starts with an exploration, in section 'Planning in the US: social conflict over property rights', of the relationship between property rights and public planning in the US, and especially the tools of the latter – zoning and subdivision rules – that play an important role in American planning practices. After this, the focus is on Houston, which is known for its atypical regulatory practice (in Section 'Houston: no zoning, but not unregulated'). This is followed (in Section 'Houston city planning in practice: Montebello'), as in Chapters 4 and 5, by a description of the development process of a housing site – Montebello – and a transaction-cost analysis thereof (in Section 'Houston city planning in practice: Montebello').

## Planning in the US: social conflict over property rights

As in the Netherlands, and hence unlike England, in the US the concept of both *dominium* and *imperium* has an important position in written legislation, more specifically in the constitution. The United States does not have a national land law that defines the reach of private property. For land use planning and property rights in land, the most important part of federal law is to be found in the last clause of the Fifth Amendment to the US Constitution dating from 1791, also known as the taking clause, which is phrased as: 'nor shall private property be deprived for public use, without just compensation'. This phrase has had an enormous effect on planning and the restriction of private property rights at the local level. In addition, it has been the subject of much discussion and controversy in and outside the courtroom. In the beginning the meaning was clear (Jacobs 1998), because a taking was seen as physical claim on land for public purposes, like schools, parks, roads, etc. But public regulation of private property went further in the beginning of the twentieth century than it had gone before, most significantly after local zoning was validated by the US Supreme Court in 1926. This, in combination with arguably one of the most famous and important cases for planning – *Pennsylvania Coal Company v. Mahon* in 1922 – led to the notion that public regulation can go as far as to constitute a taking. In the case above, a state statute prohibited the underground mining of a coal company when it would cause subsidence of overlying property. The judge concluded that the costs imposed on the coal company exceeded the conveyed benefits for the homeowners, which made it a taking of rights from the coal company. These kinds of takings have become known as 'regulatory takings'.

Apart from this federal jurisprudence, most land use regulations are established and implemented at the state and the local level. When the three countries are compared to each other, the USA (which is typical for federal states) is most decentralised with regard to land use planning, England is most centralised and the Netherlands has an intermediary position with its concept of the 'decentralised unitary state'. Nevertheless, subdivision regulations have become widespread throughout the whole US, zoning regulations likewise, except for one big city – Houston (Texas).

## Zoning: the number one tool in the US

Zoning is one of the most (and probably *the* most) important planning tools in the United States. Before zoning was introduced, there were basic building regulations and nuisance rules to solve problems of health, safety and nuisance. First, they differ from zoning in that zoning can be applied differently within a city depending on the particular location, and second that zoning is directed to control future development instead of existing use problems (Cullingworth, 1997, pp. 59–60).

New York City is regarded as the first city to adopt a comprehensive zoning ordinance in 1916. In 1924, the federal Advisory Committee on Building Codes and Zoning, appointed by the Secretary of State, drafted a Standard State Zoning Enabling Act, which was intended as model for the state zoning ordinances. As the limits of public intervention were unclear, it was found necessary by the Secretary of State to carefully draft a universal act that is in accordance with the Constitution. This would allow states to make ordinances that were not likely to be judged unjust by the courts. This proved to be a great success. In 1926, 42 states had adopted a zoning ordinance, based on this federal act.

The Euclid case in 1926, in which the Supreme Court dealt with the zoning ordinance in the village of Euclid, actually gave zoning its constitutionality as a tool to discriminate between locations. This case had a significant impact on the applicability of zoning. Zoning was no longer just an upgraded nuisance rule, but could be used to separate uses from each other, particularly industry, shops and apartments from single-family dwellings.

> '[...] many businesses and most apartments would never have been found to be nuisances in the common law. In upholding zoning laws, the state and federal courts jettisoned the nuisance analogy, though not without some agonising about what we now call exclusionary zoning.'  (Fischel, 2004, p. 52)

Critical reviews of zoning emphasise the fact that zoning can often be exclusionary and is used to serve particular interests. That is, that of single family households living in the urban fringe. '[...] zoning is an exercise in monopoly power for the benefit of local homeowners'. (Fischel, 1978, p. 66). Two empirical illustrations that are given by Fischel are the observation that zoning tends to exclude the uses that add no or very little value to neighbouring properties, and the statement that zoning tends to restrict the supply of new (suburban) housing in metropolitan areas.

In spite of much critique (e.g. Ellickson, 1973; Siegan, 1970), zoning has remained the dominant mode to regulate land use. All fifty states have passed legislation that enables local authorities to impose zoning controls, most of them based on the Standard State Zoning Enabling Act that was issued in 1924 (Cullingworth, 1997). Traditional zoning, also called Euclidian zoning – which designates and often separates land uses – has been supplemented and sometimes even replaced by new forms that have emerged under labels such as design-based, performance, overlay and incentive zoning. Although all these forms are planning tools that serve an instrumental purpose, they also have a symbolic value. This has become particularly clear in the discussions on the adoption of zoning in Houston (see Section 'Houston: no zoning, but not unregulated'), which were generally held in an emotional and ideological fashion (Buitelaar, forthcoming).

## Subdivision as second best

Subdivision regulations are rules for minimum lot sizes, building lines and parking availability. Originally, the aim of this power was to divide a tract of land into two or more parcels in order to facilitate the establishment of clear titles and hence to simplify land transactions (Cullingworth, 1997, p. 73). One could say that it was introduced to reduce transaction costs. But, from the early twentieth century onwards, its applicability as a planning tool has significantly broadened. According to Ben-Joseph (2003, p. 15) three general goals can be distinguished for the imposition of such subdivision regulations nowadays:

> 'preventing premature partial subdivisions which are poorly linked to the broader community; preventing poor quality substandard subdivisions with inadequate pubic facilities and infrastructure; reducing uncertainty and risk to the investor, buyer and the community.'

Seidel (1978) points to the fact that these goals have had negative impacts as well. He mentions two important factors. The first is the exclusionary impact of subdivision regulations. The desire for high-quality subdivisions often automatically leads, although not necessarily intentionally, to the exclusion of lower incomes. The second factor that is raised by Seidel, and which is interesting in the context of this research, is the increase of costs due to a prolonged approval process, to which I come back to in Chapter 8.

The procedures for subdivision approval are still mainly based on the standards that were established by the Federal Housing Administration (FHA) in the late 1930s and early 1940s. The process has three stages: the pre-application stage, conditional approval – or preliminary plat stage – and the stage of final plat approval. The plat review in the Houston case followed these stages as well.

## Houston: no zoning, but not unregulated

Neuman argues that: 'Houston's brand of planless planning without zoning makes it an urban planning canary, ideal for examining the government intervention versus free market debate' (2003a). The non-zoning tradition of Houston does not stand alone, it is part of the broader political and economic structure of the 'free enterprise city' – as Houston is called by Feagin (1988). This indicates an urban regime in which the local government has strong ties with the business community and tries to facilitate as many initiatives from the private sector as possible, in order to foster economic and physical growth. Exercising private property rights without much public regulation has always been a key feature of urban development in Houston. There have been several attempts to introduce zoning, but they all failed. Three referenda (in 1948, 1962 and 1993) were held in which the Houstonians could vote for the adoption of a zoning ordinance. The last election was a narrow victory for the advocates of non-zoning; they won 52 percent against 48 percent (see, Buitelaar, forthcoming, for a more elaborate exposition of the discussion on the adoption of zoning).

Attitudes towards the lack of zoning are mixed. The middle-income homeowners particularly favour zoning, because they believe that zoning prevents negative externalities and maintains property values. Others see the lack of zoning as a freedom that should promote creativity. A Steering Committee on housing[1] that wrote the report *Housing Strategies for Houston: Expanding Opportunities*, says about the absence of zoning:

> 'Unconstrained by conventional zoning regulations, Houston has a unique opportunity that no other American city has; it can under-take effective planning not trumped or compromised by existing zoning.' (p. 8)

Siegan (1970) argues that an unplanned and unzoned city of the size of Houston[2] is a good example of how the market can distribute physical space efficiently.

Houston's lack of zoning does not mean that development is unregulated (Fischel, 1985, p. 233). Although Houston does not have a comprehensive zoning ordinance (nor has Harris County of which Houston is a part), it does have subdivision controls and a building code. Moreover, Houston has adopted ordinances dealing with signs,

---

[1] In 2002, the Houston chapter of the American Institute of Architects launched an ambitious plan to help Houston with its housing policy and the great challenges/ problems it faces until 2025. Together with the Houston City Council, the business community, non-profit community-based organisations and others, they appointed a steering committee to lead that process (see www.housinghouston.org).

[2] To assess the effects of zoning on various issues, Houston has been compared several times to Dallas (Siegan, 1972; Peiser, 1981; Berry, 2001), a zoned (at least the suburban parts), but in other respects comparable city.

setbacks, pornography and the like that would typically appear in a zoning ordinance (Babcock & Siemon, 1985, pp. 263–264). One could even say that, to some extent, it is more the label of zoning that is rejected than what it is used for in most cases (Buitelaar, forthcoming). Therefore, Larson (1995, pp. 181–182) argues that Siegan's claim of Houston as a free market in land use is incorrect. Despite the lack of a zoning ordinance, there are other statutory governmental land use regulations, of which the standard subdivision regulations are the most important.

> 'Given this fact, the example hardly proves his (i.e. Siegan's) claim that land use planning is irrelevant to urban geography, affordability, or quality of life'.                (Larson, 1995, p. 182, parenthesis mine)

Nor does non-zoning imply that the planning department is not involved in city planning. The planning style of the Planning & Development Department has evolved around three principal factors (Neuman, 2003a). The first is that of large development projects mainly downtown. The second is infrastructure-led development, which means investments in the seaport, George Bush Intercontinental Airport, and light rail. And the third is that of neighbourhood planning and initiatives to facilitate homeowners' associations that use deed restrictions – a kind of private zoning – to control real property.

Siegan (1970, p. 73) explains that Houston has had a city planning department, since 1940, that operates in ways comparable to many other planning departments in other large cities. According to Siegan (1970, p. 77) the main effort of the planning department is directed towards the enforcement of the countless number of privately drafted restrictive covenants. This started in 1965 when Texan legislation was passed to allow the councils to get involved in the enforcement of residential restrictive covenants entered into privately.

## Land use regulations in Houston

The Department of Planning and Development regulates land development for Houston and its extraterritorial jurisdiction (ETJ)[3]. As Houston

---

[3] In Texas, the Local Government Code gives cities the authority to change their boundaries by annexation or disannexation of adjacent territories. Houston has a five-mile band around its boundary, in which the city has limited authority over property. One of these authorities is the imposition of Chapter 42 of the city's *Code of Ordinances*, which relates to development and subdivision of land.

is not a zoned city, the city governs development only by codes that address how land can be subdivided, and the regulations to which land use must comply in terms of, for instance, landscaping, parking, health and safety etc. In the absence of zoning, there are also regulations that have been established to regulate specific land uses. For instance, Houston has a motel/hotel ordinance, hazardous enterprises ordinance, historic preservation ordinance, manufactured homes and recreational vehicles ordinance and a tower ordinance. However, these regulations apply to the whole Houston territory and its extraterritorial belt, and are not location-specific. Private deed restrictions are the only devices that can regulate land *use* for one location specifically. I will come back to this later.

For all development, a subdivision plat needs to be submitted that indicates how the land will be subdivided. There are three platting categories, of which plat III is for the bigger commercial developments (like the case study in Section 'Houston city planning in practice: Montebello'), when the creation of a street or dedication of an easement is proposed. This process is longer and more complicated since a so-called 'joint referral process' is required, in which the abandonment of the existing easements has to be arranged (see, for more details, Section 'Houston city planning in practice: Montebello').

If land is already platted, replatting is required to further subdivide the existing subdivision plat. The plat will be reviewed by looking at whether it abides by all the regulations that are set out in Chapter 42 of the code of ordinances, the city's land development ordinance. The plat must be prepared by a licensed surveyor, land planner and/or engineer and must be signed by a licensed surveyor or engineer.

The Planning Commission[4] decides if a plat will be approved or disapproved; plats can be rejected twice. A plat cannot be rejected when it meets the requirements of Chapter 42, it then has to be approved by reason of that, and this is similar to the Dutch limited-imperative system discussed in Chapter 4. Neither can the Commission reject a plat if the Commission disagrees with the intended land use. Other issues related to the development, like sewerage, water supply and drainage, are dealt with by the department of Public Works and Engineering and do not need to be approved by the Commission. The Commission is

---

[4] The Planning Commission is a board with 25 members that is appointed by the Mayor and approved by the City Council. Besides approving subdivision plats, it also studies development issues, and on the basis of this makes recommendations to the City Council.

required (by law) to make the decision within 30 days; if it fails to do so, the plat will be automatically approved. The Department of Planning and Development will advise the Commission on approval.

A replat might require a public hearing before the Planning Commision decides. When the land is platted for single-family housing, and a replat is considered, people who live within 200 feet of the replat or within the original plat will be notified of the public hearing. If no variances from Chapter 42 are required, the Commission must approve the replat. In the case of the plat not meeting the requirements of Chapter 42, the Planning Commission has some discretionary authority to grant a variance. The applicant must document 'reasonable hardship' to support the variance, which would usually mean that he must prove that the land would be undevelopable without the variance. People living within 250 feet of the plat will be notified of proposed variances and get a chance to deliver input on how the variance could affect neighbourhood properties.

After a (re-)plat is submitted and approved, a property owner must apply for a building permit. This is done by submitting a site plan, which is required for all buildings that are built within the city. This requirement also applies to the remodelling of buildings when this changes the footprint of the structure. The plan will be reviewed on its conformity with the building code (Chapter 10) and other related codes. The site plan must include parking (Chapter 26), landscaping (Chapter 33), building lines and setbacks. During the review, plans are also checked for water and wastewater capacity (Chapter 47), drainage and infrastructure (Chapter 44). These reviews are carried out by the Department of Public Works and Engineering's Code Enforcement Division[5].

## Deed restrictions[6] in Houston[7]

The most important legal restrictions for land use control are restrictive covenants, which are private agreements among property owners as to how the land may be used. The City of Houston describes (in the Deed Restrictions Compliance Notice) deed restrictions as: '[...]

---

[5] Until October 2004 this division was part of the Department of Planning and Development. Over the years it has bounced between both departments.

[6] In the literature, restrictive covenants, deed restrictions and deed covenants are used interchangeably.

[7] This section draws to some extent from Berry (2001).

written agreements that restrict or limit the use or activities that may take place on a property in a subdivision'.

The restrictions appear in the real property records of the county of Harris, in which the property is located, and they run with the land in order to restrict future owners accordingly. The most common use of deed restrictions is by neighbouring land owners of residential property on various aspects of land use, like the type of use, the number of structures, lot size, living space, height, setback, maintenance, and number of occupants. There are limits to the kind of conditions can be imposed. For instance, racially exclusionary conditions are not legally enforceable. Until 1948 they were widely used, when the US Supreme Court declared them unenforceable in the case *Shelly V. Kraemer.*

In Harris County, over 10 000 deed restricted plats are recorded and registered with the county, of which two-thirds are for residences, covering many more – more than 10 000 – properties. Developers of subdivisions often set up deed restrictions and impose them, through the property transaction, on the first residents. To draw up restrictive covenants in developed areas is more complicated and costly, since all property owners need to accept the change voluntarily (McDonald, 1995). After the covenants have been established they are usually monitored and overseen by the neighbourhood residents; often developers take the initiative to install homeowner associations to do this. The covenants are usually renewed automatically, mostly every 20 to 30 years, unless a majority votes against this. Creating or modifying deed restrictions can be a labour-intensive exercise, as usually much time has to be spent on gathering neighbourhood support (www.houstontx.gov/planning).

In conjunction with the widespread use of deed restrictions, Houston has many neighbourhoods that organise themselves around these deed restrictions. It is famous for its *master-planned communities.* No metropolitan area in the country has more master-planned communities than Houston (www.window.state.tx.us) (interview with Atef Sharkawy). Master-planned communities are privately planned and managed sites (which can be enormous) with many facilities (like schools, malls, leisure etc.) and hence different land uses. It is argued that, largely due to the lack of zoning, people feel the need to regulate themselves within a community. To support this, the City of Houston has set up the Neighborhood Technical Assistance Center (NTAC), to help neighbourhood-based organisations by providing information of various kinds and by providing training. In addition, the Planning and Development Department has a deed restrictions development program, which assists neighbourhoods in creating, renewing or updating deed restrictions and educates them on the value of deed restrictions, particularly for keeping commercial activities out of residential areas. It provides these services for free, under the Deed Restrictions Pro Bono Program, to neighbourhoods that have properties with a value under $110 000.

Deed restrictions are widely used throughout the US. What makes Houston special is that they are not used in conjunction with zoning and that state legislation has been passed that allows the city to enforce the private agreements. After the rejection of zoning in the 1962 referendum, there was pressure to enhance the power of the local government in another way (Berry, 2001). As deed restrictions were the main instrument for land use regulation, it was found appropriate for the city to gain more influence in enforcing covenants. In 1965, two new articles (974a-1 and 974a-2) were passed and included in the Texas legislature, referred to as the Restrictive Covenant Enforcement Acts.

The first article provides cities without a zoning ordinance with the possibility of enforcing private restrictive covenants. It also prescribes that no authority can interfere with these private agreements, unless at least one covenanter submits an official complaint to the city. The City of Houston restricted itself further, by adopting a city ordinance in which it is said that restrictions are only allowed to be enforced by the city when *land use* restrictions are violated, but not for violations of setback, number, or size restrictions. In practice, the city has been reluctant to use its enforcement powers; the homeowners associations have remained the primary enforcers[8].

Article 974a-2 has had more practical consequences. Usually, granting or rejecting a building permit happens independently of deed restrictions. So, although a restriction might be violated by a building permit, it is not a consideration that is allowed to be taken into account. The situation in Houston, and Texas in general, is different from the rest of the US, as 974a-2 enables any city of more than 900 000 inhabitants to refuse a building permit if it violates a registered deed (Henderson, 1987).

In line with this, the City of Houston has issued (in 2004), a Deed Restriction Compliance Notice, in which it notifies all citizens of

---

[8] In an interview with the legal department, I was told that the deed restrictions enforcement team employs only four people. Enforcement occurs only on the basis of complaints.

Houston that all building permits 'will be verified for deed restrictions'. In addition, the notice informs citizens about the penalties that could be given as the result of non-compliance:

> 'You may not purchase a building permit without signing a sworn deed restriction affidavit stating that you are aware of and agree to abide deed restrictions pertaining to your project. If you knowingly or unknowingly sign the deed restriction affidavit under false pretences, you could be subject to municipal court citations, fines, and the removal of the structure or violating portion thereof.'

When people apply for a building permit, a deed restrictions affidavit has to be filled out in which the owner (or his agent) affirms that there are no deed restrictions, or none that will be violated by the requested permit, on the property.

## Houston city planning in practice: Montebello

Montebello is a luxury condominium complex of 30 stories, near Post Oak Boulevard and ringway 610, which is Southwest of downtown Houston (see Figure 6.1 for the location).

It consists of 112 units, 268 parking spaces underneath the building (which is rare in Houston), all kinds of luxurious facilities, a swimming pool, a fitness area etc. It has been developed by Interfin Companies, that completed the building in the summer of 2004. Montebello was not the only building in this development by Interfin; an almost identical building (Villa d'Este) was built, as well as an Italian style shopping centre, and a hotel that is under construction at the moment of writing.

Post Oak Boulevard and Montebello are part of the Galleria area[9] – also called uptown Houston – which is mainly a large business/office area that has attracted many new developments, sometimes at the expense of downtown. To guarantee and protect the high standards (i.e. the high property values) of Post Oak Boulevard and retain the clientele (including George Bush Sr), the Uptown Houston

---

[9] The Galleria area is put forward as being one of the earliest and clearest examples of an edge city in Garreau's (1988) famous book *Edge City: Life On The New Frontier.*

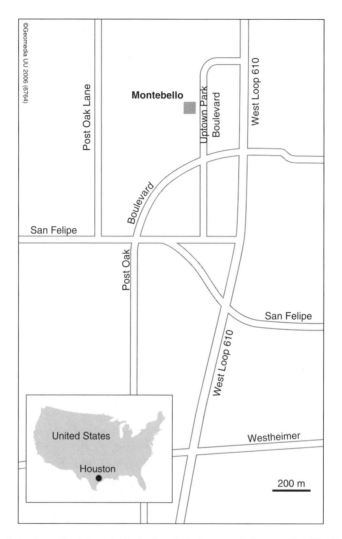

**Figure 6.1**    Location Montebello in the Galleria area © Geomedia UU 2006 (6764).

Association was founded in 1975.[10] The association was founded to serve mainly business interests or, as the website says (www.uptown-houston.com):

---

[10] This was done by Gerald Hines, who developed (among others) the Galleria (a big shopping mall) and the Williams Tower, which is the highest office tower in the world (275 meters) outside a central business district. Currently, John Breeding runs the Association as executive director (interview Suzy Hartgrove).

'To address the challenges facing the area's growth. The Uptown Houston Association strives to coordinate area-wide planning, to focus on the implementation of area improvements and to serve as a forum for area business interests.'

Since residential functions and retail entered the area, the Uptown Houston Association (UHA) can be seen more as an urban association with the goal to beautify the area. All the property owners pay a fee on a yearly basis. The UHA takes care of, for instance, traffic measures beyond those of the city, it interacts with the government, organises security, promotes the area and so on.

Almost ten years ago, the association received the status of a TIRZ (Tax Increment Reinvestment Zone). This is a program of the state of Texas that allows the area to gain a portion of the property tax that is levied after a new development is completed. Then the Uptown Houston Association can issue bonds, which it has done so far to a total of 15 million dollars, (and it will be able to issue the enormous amount of 100 million dollars in the next 15 years). With this money, the Uptown Houston Association has upgraded the area with stainless steel traffic light poles, stainless steel arches above the streets, more exclusive landscaping and all sorts of amenities. The offices, housing and retail are therefore at the higher end of the market.

The development process of Montebello can be divided into several stages that follow roughly the same sequence as described by a chart (see Figure 6.2) that was published by the taskforce for building permits (appointed by the mayor). In this chart, we also see an indication of the general duration of each stage. Due to site-specific features, the phasing of Uptown Park and the situation on the real estate

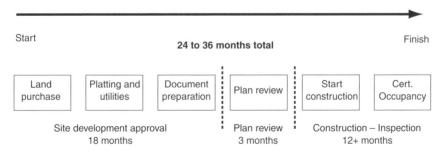

**Figure 6.2**   An average development process in Houston (The Mayor's Building Permit Taskforce, 2004, edited version).

market at the time the land was bought, this is not a completely accurate time estimate for Montebello. Nevertheless, the total time of around three years is close to the time spent on the development process of Montebello, in relation to the dynamics in the user rights regime.

Before the land was bought, Houston was recovering from a major crisis in the1980s, due to two simultaneous and interrelated events. One was the crash of the oil industry; in 1982 the price of oil was $0.40 per gallon and in 1984 it was $0.08. Due to the booming oil prices before 1982, the city was booming too, as was the real estate market, which led to many buildings being built in the 1970s and early 1980s. So when the oil industry fell, other sectors, such as the property sector, did too. It was even worse for the property sector as it was in the middle of a boom when, all of a sudden – as one of the interviewees said – 'there was no-one there any more to buy the property': around 250 000 people left Houston in just two years. It took ten years (from 1984–1994) to recover from that depression.

The land (24 acres), on which Villa d'Este, Montebello, the hotel and the shopping centre were built (see Figure 6.1), was bought in 1992 from the US government. The property was put into a special government real estate entity called RTC (Resolution Trust Corporation), which receives assets – like real estate – that are part of the savings and loans of people and organisations that went broke. Originally, the site was developed for single-family homes (30 large tracts of land). But, before Interfin came in, Superior Oil had bought and demolished the houses. It wanted to build office buildings, but the Houston economy and real estate market was not receptive at that time. Then Superior Oil sold the land to a real estate speculator, who then got into troubles, after which the land ended up with the lender, after which it was passed on to the RTC. RTC wanted to dispose of the land in 1992, but not many were interested in buying land in Houston at that time. Interfin was very interested, as it was almost in the backyard of its office, and because it was relatively cheap for the location. This well-known edge city had seen prosperous times and, because of its very good accessibility, it was expected that it would soon regain its potential. Interfin bought the land (relatively cheaply), knowing that there was enough development potential, as it was so close to the freeway and as it was part of Post Oak Boulevard, an area with a high status. What helped in this respect was that Interfin was already familiar with the area, as they had already built Four-Leaf Towers and Four Oaks Place: six office towers in total.

After the transaction of the property title, a due diligence of 60 days started in order to allow environmental experts to investigate whether there was any soil contamination and to do a land survey. The experts also looked at (i.e. quickly scanned for) necessary elevations that are necessary in case the property is on a flood plain. No preliminary plat was submitted, as Interfin wanted to buy the land anyway[11]. The contract had already been signed, but if Interfin had found something unwanted or suspicious it could have walked away from the purchase, or renegotiated the price. Nothing special (although a small part of the site was on a floodplain) was found during the period that could break up the agreement.

After the land was bought in1992, Interfin spent approximately two years planning and thinking about what they wanted to do with it, and geting the plat approved. A team of consultants came on board. Interfin took its time, since the market did not seem ready at that moment for high-rise condominiums.

Years before Interfin bought the land, it had been a subdivided land for single-family housing (30 tracts in total), and when Interfin bought the land it was still platted in that way. It decided to subdivide the land into five pieces (not knowing exactly what to do with it), in order to put condominiums, retail and a hotel on it. The piece on which Montebello was built, like the other four subdivisions, was subdivided as an 'unrestricted reserve', which means that it is:

'[…] a parcel of land that is not a lot, but is created within a subdivision plat for other than single-family residential use and is established to accommodate some purpose for which a division into lots is not suitable or appropriate.'
                    (p. 2869 of Chapter 42 of the Code of Ordinances)

In addition, it wanted to lay out a street (now Uptown Park Boulevard) to connect the freeway to Post Oak Boulevard.

The whole Uptown Park site was platted as a class III plat, which is a category that usually applies to the bigger developments as these are subdivisions that require or propose (1) the creation of any new street,

---

[11] Potential buyers of land are allowed to submit a preliminary application when they consider buying land for purchase. In many cases the purchase is dependent on the result of the review of that application (see www.houstontx.gov).

or/and (2) the dedication of any easement for public water, wastewater collection or storm sewer lines, and/or (3) it regards a vacating plat (one that vacates all or a portion of previously platted property). All three requirements applied to the Uptown Park subdivision. A class III plat requires a submittal in two stages, a preliminary and a final plat. Objections from adjacent property owners should be made during this preliminary submittal process, but in this case there were no objections. Interfin submitted the application after the land had been purchased. After the preliminary plat is submitted, it ideally takes nine days for the staff of the Planning and Development Department to review the plats and make recommendations to the Planning Commission. The Department reviews the plat for streets, lot sizes, set back lines, open space requirements, parking etc. In the instance of a preliminary plat, and presuming it meets the requirements of Chapter 42, it will ideally be approved on day ten (from an interview with Suzy Hartgrove).

Besides the review by the Department of Planning and Development, the plat was also sent to the Department of Public Works and Engineering. The Department did two things at this stage. First, it looked to see if there were any major impediments to the capacity of the public utilities such as water supply, wastewater collection and treatment, and storm drainage. As the site comprised 24 acres, the development was considered a major impediment. The Planning and Development Commission took the outcome of this review into consideration, by making reference to the Wastewater Capacity Reservation letter that needed to be obtained. The Public Works Department also reviews for easement abandonments. Some easements can be abandoned simply by the replat, but in the case of public utilities (i.e. public rights of way), as in this case, a joint referral process is required. The preliminary plat of Uptown Park was approved by the Planning and Development Department subject to a joint referral process. Then the final plat was submitted taking into account the comments that were tied to the approval of the preliminary plat. The plat was then again reviewed by the two earlier mentioned departments and was approved and recorded in October 1992, subject (again) to the joint referral process. The time taken for the platting procedure was around three months, which includes the preparation done by Interfin and its advisors.

The joint referral process is a process in which the joint referral committee of the City of Houston is requested to abandon or sell a street, alley, or easement that is owned by the City. Interfin had to hire a civil engineering firm to survey the existing roads and easements. It also calculated the acreage that Interfin wanted to buy from the city. In the calculation, following the new plan, Interfin also gave land back to the city, and this had to be included in the equation. According to city charts, this process could take up to 40 weeks, and that is the time spent on the joint referral process at Uptown Park.

Besides the provision and exchange of space for utilities on site, in the form of a joint referral, the connection to and capacity of the City's utility network has to be bought, by paying impact fees. The city uses a ratio of type and use for calculating how much utility capacity you have to buy when you want to build on your land. It calculates how many square feet of, for instance, office building translates into gallons of water a day. You have to buy this capacity from the sewage treatment plant, through Public Works and Engineering. Superior Oil had already bought the capacity[12] and the letter that confirmed that it ran with the land. The application for utility capacity is usually made simultaneously with the joint referral and platting process. At Uptown Park, the platting, utility and joint referral process together took one year.

After the original (re)plat in 1992, the subdivision was replatted twice, in June 1994 and in November 2000. The first time was because Interfin had the chance to acquire an additional piece of land to add onto the site in order to extend the retail centre. On this new site there was a creek or bayou. It was enclosed in large concrete boxes underneath the ground. This was Interfin's initiative and was not required by the city, although they could not have filled it up. The bayou had no environmental quality (it was more like a drainage ditch) and boxing it saved land. They had to get permits to do so from the Harris county flood control division. Nowadays, storm review is done by the City of Houston as part of the same process as the water and wastewater capacity review. The replat in November 2000 was made because the southern boundary of Montebello's subdivision had to be moved southwards in order to extend the parcel on which Montebello would be built.

After the platting and the utility/joint referral process (in 1993), schematic designs were made to explore what the buildings should look like. Around 1995, Uptown Park Boulevard and the conduit were

---

[12] It bought much more capacity than Interfin needed for its developments. But it is possible to transfer. The overcapacity now rests on a small piece of vacant land owned by Interfin. This could well be used for (and transferred to) new developments that Interfin will carry out.

built. In 1996, Villa d'Este was designed, which took around a year. In 1997, Interfin started a pre-sale marketing program to sell some units on paper, before the construction started. This was important since the banks were only prepared to pay up to 70% of the costs; so 30% equity had to come from the developers' own capital. It took about one year to get the first 30 sales contracts that were necessary to show to the bank. This took relatively long because the condominium market is a small market, and because people are not used to buying on paper. Before this pre-sale program, two to three million dollars had already been spent on consultants, advertising, marketing etc.

The construction of Villa d'Este started in 1998 and it opened in the year 2000. At the same time in 1998, the construction of the shopping centre started, which opened in 1999. The construction of Montebello started in May 2002 and it opened in June 2004. In April 2005, 90% of the development had been sold. Although Villa d'Este was an important part of the development in itself, it was also an important learning case and catalyst for Montebello. Interfin implemented the program in stages, mainly due to the earlier mentioned depression. In addition, for this type of development (high-rise condominiums) Houston only had a small market, and so the sale result was uncertain. For these reasons it was decided to plan, build and sell Villa d'Este first. Although the sale was not an instant success, after everything was sold, the market went up again, which gave Interfin enough confidence to build Montebello. The design stage of Montebello was slightly faster (less than a year) than that of Villa d'Este, since the designs of both buildings were almost identical.

When Interfin applied for a building permit for Montebello, which was the last development undertaken before the hotel, the plat was already there, but as said before the boundary had to be shifted. Then a team of architects and engineers were needed to complete a set of drawings with which Interfin could go to the city again to apply for a building permit. After the city receives a building permit like that for Montebello, a '21-day clock' for commercial[13] plan reviews starts, which is a target that the city imposes itself. After the application is received, a structural plan examiner is assigned by the Commercial Plan Review manager who oversees the review. The plan examiner

---

[13] Every plan that is not a single-family home or duplex dwelling (which are processed through a residential plan review process) is regarded as a commercial plan review.

explores the scope of the work, which department has to be involved in the review and the routing of the plan. The plan is reviewed, if all considerations are applicable, on issues such as water, sewerage, storm water drainage, floodplain, parking, health and safety.

When these elements have been checked and reviewed, the plan examiner collects all the reviews and puts the plan and the reviews in a library, awaiting review by the code enforcement division's (PWE) inspectors who examine the plan on structural, electrical, plumbing/ drainage, HVAC (heating, venting and air conditioning) and sprinkler codes. After this has been done, the plan examiner verifies all the approvals and prepares the application for permit issuance. After the applicant is granted permission, construction can begin as well as the on-site inspections for permit compliance. After the construction has been completed and carried out in line with the permit, a certificate of occupancy is issued. The application for Montebello was approved and the permit issued in June 2002. The 21-day target is not achievable for projects like Montebello, as it involves multiple condos – in this case 112 units – for which individual building permits are issued. For Montebello, it took between four and five months for the permits to come out of the review process and all the permits to be issued.

The use of Montebello is governed by deed restrictions to maintain the standard that the developer had in mind in advance. This is done through a document called 'Custom Design Criteria', set up by Interfin before the residential units were sold.  The restrictions relate to the use, alterations, decorations, maintenance etc of both residential units and the common areas[14].

## Transaction-cost analysis of Montebello

Unlike the Dutch and the English case, Montebello was not developed within the framework of a land use or zoning plan, nor did the developer enter into an agreement with the City of Houston that defined the conditions (and obligations) under which development could take place (see also Table 6.1). It was carried out within the regulations that are defined in the code of ordinances that apply to all developments within (and without) the city boundaries. There is not much discretion

---

[14] The common areas are maintained and managed, and the restrictions are enforced by a property manager.

**Table 6.1**    Transaction costs at Montebello

| Activities | Indication of the amount | Borne by |
|---|---|---|
| **1. Land exchange** | | |
| Acquisition of land from RTC | Few months (including due diligence) | **The developer** |
| Sale of the apartments | | **The developer** |
| **2. Land use or zoning plan** | | |
| Not applicable | | |
| **3. Agreement** | | |
| Not applicable | | |
| **4. Planning permission** | | |
| Subdivision plat | 3 months | **Municipality** and to a lesser extent the **developer** |
| Utilities (joint referral) | 9 months, plus several months preparations by developer | **Municipality** and to a lesser extent the **developer** |
| Planning review | 4–5 months $96,000 building fee | **Municipality**, recouped from the **developer** |
| Inspections | | **Municipality** |

for the local government to impose additional restrictions. Since the land use regulations are general and hardly vary according to the type of land use, there were very few – or no – costs involved in setting up the user rights regime of Montebello: the existing regime was used.

Altogether, the process of Montebello took around four years, which included plan preparation by Interfin, plan review by the city, construction, land acquisition and so on. However, not all activities – like platting, joint referral and utilities – were exclusively dedicated to the development of Montebello, but were applied to the whole Uptown Park area that Inferin developed between 1992 and 2005.

*Land exchange*

The acquisition of the 24 acres for Uptown Park went relatively smoothly. Interfin was very interested in the area because it had already developed many buildings there and knew the potential. At the same time RTC was happy to have a serious candidate in a period when many developers were reluctant to invest in real estate. Several months were spent on the exploration of the site. After the transaction of the property title, a due diligence of 60 days started in order to allow environmental experts to investigate whether there was any soil contamination and to do a land survey, which includes an investigation of the property titles and the plat that run with the land. The experts also looked at necessary elevations in case the property is on a flood plain. Only a small strip close to Montebello was on the flood plain, and this strip was elevated just before construction started.

The sale of the apartments of Montebello benefited greatly from the condominium complex Villa d'Este that had been developed and sold earlier. It took several years before all the units of Villa d'Este were sold, since the condominium market in Houston is small and difficult. But thereafter, it proved to be attractive, which increased the demand for Montebello. There is a growing demand for this urban lifestyle, with numerous facilities in one building. To keep up the standard, all these sorts of development are accompanied by restrictive covenants to prevent the users becoming a nuisance to one another.

## Planning permission

The stage where the user rights regime is most prominently visible is the fourth – the planning or building permission stage – where development proposals are reviewed for compliance with the city's code of ordinances. This is done in two stages, as we see in Figure 6.2. First, there is a review of the subdivision plat in conjunction with the utilities (in the joint referral process). In the case of Uptown Park (comprising the condominiums, the shopping area and the hotel), this involved the whole plat. It took over one year (including preparations by the developer) before the plat was approved and the joint referral process was completed. In addition, because of changes in the circumstances, two minor replats were required that also took around a month each. The fee that Interfin had to pay for the initial subdivision plat was around $2500.[15]

The second stage is called the 'plan review' stage, which is separate for each structure, and meant that Montebello had its own plan review process. This is the internal review procedure of the City of Houston, which took around 4 to 5 months. The preparation time spent by the developer is difficult to assess. The plan for Montebello was relatively quickly and easily drawn, as its architecture was nearly identical to that of Villa d'Este. Interfin had to pay the city a fee of around $96 000 for the building permit for Montebello.

---

[15] This amount includes the costs $1920 ($80 per acre × 24 acres) for application, and $550 for class 3 plats.

Although Houston is not unregulated, it looks quite different from the other two cases. The city is (only) involved in reviewing the proposals of the legally binding ordinances. This happens in two stages: the first soon after the land acquisition by the developer in the platting and utility stage (see also Figure 6.1), and the second just before construction starts, when the proposed structure is reviewed for compliance with building regulations. In Chapter 7, I will elaborate on the differences between the three case studies.

## References

Babcock, R. F. & Siemon, C. L. (1985) *The Zoning Game Revisited.* Lincoln Institute of Land Policy, Cambridge MA.

Ben-Joseph, E. (2003) *Subdivision Regulations: Practices and Attitudes.* Lincoln Institute of Land Policy, working paper, Boston MA.

Berry, C. (2001) Land use regulation and residential segregation: does zoning matter? *American Law and Economics Review* 3(2): 251–74.

Buitelaar, E. (forthcoming) Zoning: more than just a tool. Explaining Houston's regulatory practice, *Journal of Planning Education and Research.*

Cullingworth, B. (1997) *Planning in the USA: Policies, Issues, Processes.* Routledge, London.

Ellickson, R. C. (1973) Alternatives to zoning: covenants, nuisance rules, and fines as land use controls. *The University of Chicago Law Review* 40(4): 681–781.

Feagin, J. R. (1988) *Free Enterprise City: Houston in Political and Economic Perspective.* Rutgers University Press, New Brunswick NJ/London.

Fischel, W. A. (1978) A property rights approach to municipal zoning, *Land Economics* 54(1): 64–81.

Fischel, W. A. (1985) *The Economics of Zoning Laws.* The Johns Hopkins University Press, Baltimore MD.

Fischel, W. A. (2004) Why are judges so wary of regulatory takings. In: H. M. Jacobs (ed.), *Private Property in the 21st Century: The Future of an American Ideal,* Edward Elgar, Cheltenham (UK)/Northampton MA (USA), pp. 50–74.

The Mayor's Building Permit Task Force (2004) *Promoting Responsible Development within the City of Houston: Reforming the City's Building Permit Process.* City of Houston, Houston TX.

Garreau, J. (1988) *Edge City: Life on the New Frontier.* Doubleday, New York.

Henderson, A. (1987) Land use controls in Houston: what protection for owners of restricted property. *South Texas Law Review* 29: 131–87.

Jacobs, H. M. (ed.) (1998) *Who Owns America?: Social Conflict Over Property Rights.* The University of Wisconsin Press, Madison WI.

Larson, J. E. (1995) Free markets deep in the heart of Texas. *The Georgetown Law Journal* 84(2): 179–258.

Neuman, M. (2003a) Do plans and zoning matter? *Planning* **69**(11): 28–31.

Peiser, R. (1981) Land development regulation: a case study of Dallas and Houston, Texas. *American Real Estate and Urban Economics Association Review* **9**(4): 397–417.

Seidel, S. (1978) *Housing Costs and Government Regulations: Confronting the Regulatory Maze.* Centre for Urban Policy Research, Rutgers University, New Brunswick NJ.

Siegan, B. H. (1970) Non-zoning in Houston. *Journal of Law & Economics* **13**(1): 71–147.

Siegan, B. H. (1972) *Land Use without Zoning.* Lexington, Lexington MA.

# 7

# Comparing and Explaining Transaction Costs: Learning from the Cases

In Chapters 4, 5 and 6, we have seen three development processes that developed along different lines, leading to differences in transaction costs. In this chapter a link is made between the transaction costs and the user rights regime. These user rights regimes are connected to other institutions. Therefore, to explain transaction costs we need to look at how these user rights regimes, and the transaction costs associated with their creation and use, are embedded in a broader institutional context.

## The user rights regimes compared

There is a difference in the length of the development process between these cases. A complicating factor is, however, that all three cases were part of a bigger project, and were therefore also dependent on factors that were external to the site itself. Looking at the partial developments – but taking into account activities that related to the whole development, like land acquisition – there are still significant differences. Montebello had the fastest development process: it took approximately four years. The process started in 1992 with land acquisition, platting and a joint referral process for the whole Uptown Park site, after which the developer decided to phase the process and started with the plan preparation of Montebello as late as 2001. In 2004 the project was completed. Wapping Wharf took over six years – from the plan preparations for the land bid in 1995 until the structure was completed at the end of 2001. The Marialaan in Nijmegen was the lengthiest project of the three, with a total duration of over eight years. It started in 1994 with a joint development proposal of the developer and the municipality and ended – with the completion of the construction stage – in 2002.

Although we should be careful in drawing general conclusions from this, it is not surprising that the Dutch case had the longest span and the Houstonian case the shortest, if we look at the primary determinants of the length of the development process. The differences do not arise in the production process – like during the construction works – since this seems to be similar across these projects, but in the way the user rights regime is created and used. In Houston, existing rules – that is the city ordinances – were applied, while in the Dutch case new site-specific rules had to be made. Most time in the Dutch case was spent on the informal process of deliberation and negotiation: that took several years altogether.

Another difference between the three projects is the stage in which the transaction costs related to the user rights regime were made. In the Dutch case, most costs were made in the early plan-making stage when the formal land use plan was prepared. In Bristol, the focus is later, at the (pre-) planning application stage simultaneously with the Section 106 agreement, and even after the permission is granted, since the planning conditions required the submission of more detailed schemes in later stages. In Montebello, there was a clear split between the two most important stages. The first one was right after the land had been bought, when the developer wanted to get the development as a whole – that is the footprint – approved. The second stage was at the end of the process, when the building application for each unit of Montebello was submitted and reviewed.

Another important difference is the division of the costs between the developer and the local authority. The role of the local government was most prominent in the Dutch case, where the city of Nijmegen was involved from the very beginning, with the land acquisition, the various agreements, the schematic designs, and so on. Therefore, initially the municipality bore many transaction costs. It was, however, able to recover a large amount from the developer. In Houston, all the costs of preparing the plans and acquiring the land were borne by the developer. The only costs that the city of Houston bore were the internal costs of processing the applications and plats, of which it was able to recover a large portion from the developer. Wapping Wharf has again a middle position. Most costs were made by the developer, but the city of Bristol was considerably more involved than its Houstonian counterpart.

Especially after the planning application, the city of Bristol was involved in public consultation and negotiations about the designs and the planning obligations.

In Chapter 3, I explained the choice for investigating the development process of three housing projects, containing around 100 units in the commercial sector, assuming that this would make the case studies comparable. However, this assumption may have been too simplistic since the projects proved to be quite different, not only in terms of the way the process was organised, but also with regard to the initial starting point – the nature and location of the site – and to events that occurred. Remediableness (see Chapter 2) is a difficult criterion for judging the performance of various institutional arrangements in terms of transaction costs. Although all three projects have a comparable output – namely apartment blocks of around 100 non-subsidised units – there are many other variables that make comparison extremely difficult. Examples of these variables are: the nature of the site, fragmentation of ownership, the nature of the stakeholders and external processes.

In addition, transaction costs cannot just be attributed to institutions or governance structures, but are the result of interplay between these structures and the subjects. User rights regimes are created and used by agents and do not produce any transaction costs on their own. Comparing micro institutions on their transaction costs, like the remediableness criterion suggests, therefore becomes illusive. In addition, the room for manoeuvre is constrained by the rules of the game that are made at a higher level, the meso institutions. Rules with regard to land use and exchange, from both private and public law, limit the number of options at the site level.

The cases have demonstrated very different ways in which user rights regimes are created and used. The table (Table 3.2) I used in Chapter 3, with possible transaction-cost generation factors, related to the creation and the use of the user rights regime, and I have used it as a guideline to analyse the case studies (Table 7.1). In this chapter, I will look at the relevance of these factors and the differences between the three case studies.

## Land exchange

The way the land was acquired for the development in the three case studies differs on several points. In the case of Montebello and

**Table 7.1**   Possible transaction-cost generating factors with creating and using the user rights regimes (see also Buitelaar 2004).

| Moments/stages in the development process where the user rights regime is created and/or used | Possible transaction-cost generating factors |
|---|---|
| 1. Land exchange | – number of parties involved and the number of parcels exchanged<br>– conflict of interest<br>– information about future possibilities<br>– delineation (assignment) of rights<br>– and the information of the delineation of rights: land registry or not<br>– use of hierarchical means (for example, compulsory purchase, pre-emption rights) |
| 2. Making land use or zoning plan/building ordinance etc. (i.e. regulations of land use) | – stakeholder participation<br>– appeal<br>– number of parties involved<br>– conflict of interest<br>– structure of the plan: legally binding – indicative<br>– structure of the procedure: administrative – political |
| 3. Agreement (between for example, developer and municipality) | – number of parties involved<br>– conflict of interest<br>– structure of agreement / contract: detailed – flexible |
| 4. Planning permission | – yes, no, or conditional<br>– number of parties involved<br>– conflict of interest<br>– possibility of negotiation (planning gain)<br>– possibility of appeal and the actual use of it<br>– structure of the procedure: administrative – political<br>– structure of the permission: conditional – unconditional |

Wapping Wharf, there was only one owner from whom land had to be acquired, respectively RTC and British Rail. The Marialaan site embraced two parcels, one owned by a gas station and one by a builders' merchant. This made the land acquisition more complex and transaction-cost consuming. This was also influenced by the fact that there was a viable land use – that is the builders' merchant – at the Marialaan before the development of the site, while the land in the other cases was derelict and vacant. Therefore, the municipality of Nijmegen had to search for a new spot to relocate the builders' merchant, which led to additional transaction costs, in the form of acquisition costs.

Reviewing the three cases, it also seems as if the chance of conflict of interest increases when more landowners involved. The developer of the Marialaan could not come to an agreement for the Northern part of the MVK triangle, which led to a re-delineation and subdivision of the project boundaries. But this fragmentation led to an increase in the transaction costs since many activities (like producing a *bestemmingsplan*) have to be done twice.

In all three cases, no hierarchical means to acquire land were used by the local authority. In Houston, this was not necessary since the developer was able to acquire the land easily. In addition, the city hardly ever uses expropriation, due to its general reluctance to interfere with the individual freedom to do with the land whatever the landowner pleases. In the English case, it was not necessary for the initial land acquisition to use compulsory purchase because British Rail – the landowner – was one of the partners involved in the redevelopment of Harbourside. However, in order to acquire the land to operate the electric bus, it might have been helpful if expropriation had been applied. But it is complex and costly, and therefore it is rarely used in Bristol. The benefits of the electric bus did not seem to outweigh the costs of an induced land sale. This also counts for the Dutch case, where compulsory purchase would have been expensive and probably lengthy. It was possible to start with at least part of the development using amicable acquisition.

Before a developer buys land and property he wants to have a fair degree of certainty – to minimise development risks – about the future possibilities. These possibilities are constrained and demarcated by the land use regulations that are set by the local authority. Developers try to acquire as much information as they can about what they will be allowed to develop. In the Houston case, nearly everything was known in advance, since the code of ordinances includes almost all the regulations. To reduce uncertainty even more, one can decide to submit a preliminary plat, an opportunity Interfin did not take because it wanted to buy and develop the site anyway. For the Dutch site, it was clear that what the developer wanted to build was not possible under the existing user rights regime. But the municipality agreed to cooperate to change the regime, and to buy an additional piece of land, in order to accommodate housing development. However, the volume, density, number of units and many other details were not completely worked out before the land was bought. The developer had to rely on the willingness of the city of Nijmegen. At Wapping Wharf, the user rights regime was less clear to the developer, except for the fact that the local plan designated the land for housing. The local planning authority had a large degree of discretionary power to determine the content of the planning permission, the conditions and the obligations.

Looking at how the property rights were defined, from a private law perspective, there are not many differences between the cases that could give rise to transaction costs. The Netherlands, England and the US all have a system of land registry; the first two have national cadastres, while in the US property records are local matters. However, it seems as if the English case was a bit more complex and transaction-cost consuming, due to some uncertainties about ownership and the division of rights: something that could be explained by the feudal property rights tradition, which leads to a situation with multiple interests. Everything should be recorded, but in practice this does not always seem to be the case. In addition, it is only since 1990 that access to information from the Land Registry was granted to the public. But still, details of prices remain confidential (Adams *et al.*, 2002).

Applying transaction cost theory, one could say the land was acquired in all cases through relational governance structures. As already mentioned, expropriation, compulsory purchase or eminent domain were neither necessary nor used. But neither can we speak of market structures, in the classical sense of competitive markets with many buyers and sellers that have transient exchanges and no mutual relationships. In these cases, the land exchange was preceded by negotiation and the building of a relationship between the parties involved. The land acquisition – at least if land is acquired by private parties – is often informed by the information provided by the hierarchical structures in place, like land use plans or development ordinances. However, the choice for the governance structures is not a choice from an unlimited number of alternatives. First, this choice is constrained by the public and private rules that arrange land exchange. But in addition, the actions with regard to land acquisition are influenced by and embedded in the relationship with the initial landowner, past experiences (for example, with the use of compulsory purchase), conventions and so on, which in their turn are embedded in social structures. Therefore, transaction costs cannot be voluntarily optimised or reduced, but are dependent on and influenced by institutions at different levels. I come back to this in Section 'Transaction costs entangled in structures' and Chapter 8.

### Land use or zoning plan

Houston is a city without a plan, and therefore, there were no transaction costs involved in making a land use or zoning plan. However, there were obviously costs involved in making the city's development ordinance and other land use related ordinances. For instance, all the lobbying, public consultation, and referenda in 1948, 1962 and 1993 – and before and after –brought about many costs. These costs are dispersed, though, among the thousands of developments that are carried out in the city. Something similar can be said about the local plan in England, which was made not only for Wapping Wharf but for the whole city. The planning briefs from 1995 and 1998 were more closely related to the development, since these were specific for to the whole Harbourside area. The local plan – if one takes into account that it is an indicative plan – was, however, a costly plan preceded by a lengthy process, and its validity was limited. The plan was finished in 1997, after a five year process of discussions and public consultation, and it planned four years ahead until 2001.

In the Dutch case, the land use plan had a much more prominent position than in the other two cases, since the new plan was made for the site and because it was legally binding. The plan procedure itself was a standard administrative procedure that took one year. The constraints for this procedure were set by the meso-level institutions, especially the planning act (WRO). In this process, there were certain formalised moments for public consultation. There were not many objections, and this allowed the process to run relatively smoothly at that stage. The preparation of the formal plan before the procedure was complex and time-consuming. It took up to five years before it was ready to enter the *bestemmingsplan* procedure and to be formally agreed in the development agreement. This was a process that was intimately linked with drawing up and negotiating the intention and the development agreement. One of the factors behind the length of the process was the close involvement of the municipality in the process from the very beginning. One consequence was that the municipality got involved in details and issues (for example, the choice of the architect) that in many other countries are considered to be the task of the developer. This fits within a planning culture in which the state traditionally – since the beginning of the twentieth century – plays a central role (see Section 'Transaction costs entangled in structures'). The other way in which the involvement of the municipality affected the length of the process is the time that had to be spent building and maintaining a good relationship, to discuss and to negotiate the plans, which fits within the Dutch corporatist tradition. The city used hierarchical governance structures (that is, its power to change and determine the land use plan) as a stick in order to strengthen its control over the development. This was mainly used to steer the content of the plans and to reduce the municipality's own financial involvement, and not so much to steer the length of the development process or to control the total project costs. This is related to the attitude of the Dutch municipalities towards transaction costs in general. The difference in attitude of local authorities (in the three countries) towards transaction costs is also something that is embedded in a planning and development culture, and will also be discussed in Section 'Transaction costs entangled in structures' and Chapter 8.

*Agreement*

Once again, there were no agreements signed between the developer and the city of Houston: this rarely occurs at the project level, except for some major downtown redevelopments. In England, Section 106 agreements are statutory agreements that are used to deal with neighbourhood facilities in order to mitigate the possible damage done by the development to the surroundings. One of the obligations in the Bristol case was the improvement of a junction nearby, and another the construction of combined cycle and foot path. It took around seven months before the agreement was signed and permission granted. Compared to the Dutch case this is a very short process, since there it took approximately five years from the first discussion till the final development agreement. It must be noted that while these processes were going on, schemes were being drawn up and calculations made. One of the main reasons for this relatively long time span in Nijmegen was the discussion in the early stages of the project. Trust was an important mechanism that kept the developer and the city together, but at the same time it seemed to prevent both parties from doing business, since that could have harmed the relationship.

The agreements in both Bristol and Nijmegen can be seen (see also Chapter 2) as relational governance structures under the shadow of hierarchy. For both cases, the local authority could ultimately withhold permission for the development in the case of non-compliance. However, this similarity does not mean that the transaction costs are the same. In the Dutch case, many costs that were incurred through the preparation were shared more equally since all elements were mutually agreed upon. In Bristol, most of the costs were borne by the local authority, since it is the city council that wants the developer to perform certain tasks. However, as we will see in Chapter 8, in both England and the Netherlands there are ways of transferring the costs to the developer.

### Planning permission

The planning permission stage in the Netherlands is formalised, technical and hierarchical, and there is very little room for politics. It is an administrative exercise in which the plans are reviewed for compliance with all the appropriate conditions (for example the *bestemmingsplan*). The same counts for Houston, where the plans for Montebello were reviewed for conformity with the building code, health codes, water, waste water and so on.

The situation in Bristol was quite different, because after the planning application was submitted, the development process entered a very political stage, due to the central location of the site and the nature of English development control (something I will come back to, in the next Section 'Transaction costs entangled in structures'). In England there are targets; applications should be determined within eight or thirteen weeks. In the case of Wapping Wharf this target was thirteen weeks. The review of the application for Wapping Wharf, however, took seven months (together with the Section 106 agreement). Within these seven months – in the absence of a legally binding plan – all decisions with regard to the appropriate development (that is, the most important land use decisions) had to be made. However, because this is still a rather short time span, the city postponed many detailed decisions to later stages, by imposing conditions that require the submission of more detailed proposals later in the development process.

If we look at the role of participation in the planning permission stage, we see an especially interesting example in Wapping Wharf. As it is often said (see e.g. Webster, 2005, pp. 53–54) that public participation can raise the transaction costs in the development process significantly. In the Dutch case, some months were spent (some would say lost) in redesigning the plan, by reducing the volume and adding a garage. However, when public opinion is not taken seriously, something which seems to have happened at Wapping Wharf, the consequences for the transaction costs can be even worse. The plan was rejected and had to be redrawn and recalculated, communicated with the neighbourhood and resubmitted[1]. It is remarkable that the developer let this happen, because Wapping Wharf has a prominent and eye-catching position in the city, combined with a design that is at odds with traditional English (Georgian) architecture. In contrast, the Marialaan is situated in an area that is in need of regeneration, and spatial and financial injections. In addition, it has a rather average architecture, which would make it less controversial. In the end, in neither case were there third party appeals that could have increased the costs even further.

## Transaction costs entangled in structures

As we saw in Chapters 4, 5 and 6, there are transaction costs that are incurred because of requirements imposed from higher tiers of government, such as certain procedures that need to be followed or instruments that can and/or have to be used. In addition, the situation at the site, for example, land ownership, has a strong influence on the way the development process is carried out and how this affects transaction costs. This means that we cannot change and create governance structures for a particular project, and thereby reduce transaction costs, as we would like. Institutions are path dependent and situated in an institutional framework, as discussed in Chapter 2. For actors at the level of location development, it is difficult to change structures at higher levels, such as those of the national, regional and sometimes even the municipal level.

Despite those constraints, institutions (at the micro level) are social constructions, with room for agents to design them. Many transaction costs are the result of the way in which the user rights regimes are constructed and used at the site level. Why did it take so long before the city of Nijmegen and the developer reached a decision? Why did the Bristol City Council impose so many conditions? Why was the city of Houston so passive with regard to Montebello? In this light the assumptions I made in Table 7.1 and 3.2 acknowledge too little institutions as social constructions. As said before, the transaction costs are not solely caused by, for instance, the rules for a procedure or

---

[1]   In another research (Buitelaar *et al.* 2006), we also saw a Dutch example of a project – the Hofpoort – in the city of Arnhem, which showed that neglecting the opinion of the public can cause serious delays and increases in transaction costs.

public consultation, but also by the way these are mainly used. Personal characteristics are important for the way these institutions are used. The developer in the English case, for instance, emphasised the importance of the changes in staff, both on the side of the developer and the city of Bristol. This decreased the 'collective memory' and increased transaction costs. Another example is the importance of Georgio Borlenghi, the director of the developer in the Houston case: he led the project through all the stages. In other words, agents can make a difference.

However, many of the decisions with regard to the developments do not stand on their own and are often not the result of fluid and transient behaviour, but are embedded in social structures and cultural settings, which are reproduced (or challenged) by those actions. Transaction cost economics assumes that agents are aware (within the limits of bounded rationality) of the transaction costs they bear, and as a result of that, search for the governance structures that economise most on transaction costs. But this research demonstrates (see also Section 'Attitudes towards transaction costs') that there are different degrees of transaction cost awareness. More generally, transaction cost economics takes very little account of the institutional context; it literally regards it 'as a given' (Williamson, 1996, p. 5). The cases have shown that many differences in the way user rights regimes are created and used, and the transaction costs that are related to that, are strongly intertwined with the institutional context – in this case the macro institutions – in which they are situated.[2]

On the basis of the findings from Chapters 4, 5 and 6, the comparison in Section 'The user rights regions compared', and additional literature, I have identified four (interrelated) dimensions of the macro level that I will briefly describe here, and that will be elaborated in more detail in Chapter 8. The (spatial) level at which an institution is analysed depends on its relevance and is therefore not necessarily the same for all cases. For instance, in the case of Houston, planning practice will often be placed in the context of Houston's urban regime, while in the case of the Netherlands, and even more so in England, the national context provides many leads for explanation. In the case of the US – a

---

[2] Once again, the word 'context' (or 'environment') might suggest that these institutions are external to the site and influence / structure the actions in the project exogenously. The duality of structure is explicitly acknowledged here, without entirely conflating both.

federal state – local autonomy and diversity is greater, which makes the specific urban regime a relevant context. England and the Netherlands are nation-states, which makes the urban regime not always the only appropriate level of analysis (Wood, 2004).

## *The quest for control over development*

The first category deals with the quest for control (Van Gunsteren, 1976). Planning is – beside other functions – an *instrument of control* (Friedmann, 2003). However, the way in which, and the extent to which countries, regions and localities exercise control varies.

If there is only one party that wants to control, there will not be any conflicting interest and hence the transaction costs will be relatively low. Obviously a developer wants to increase his control over a development as much as possible, in order to reduce risk and uncertainty, so as to increase his returns on investment. In many cases, governments also have a desire to control development. The directive role of the city of Nijmegen fits within the Dutch planning culture. This role, and also the level of detail in which agencies want to exercise it, have had their consequences for the transaction costs not only at the Marialaan, but also in many other cases. Because of the involvement of the municipality, many meetings were held with the developer, on the choice of the architect, the design, materials and so on. The situation is entirely different in Houston, where the local government stays at a distance. Only a few meetings were held in which a local officer explained what the requirements of the city were. Therefore, specific attention has to be given to the wish of local governments to control, and how that bears on transaction costs.

## *Relationship public and private sector*

What we have also seen in the three cases, as an important factor behind the transaction costs and their incidence, is the relationship between the local authority and the developer, or in more general terms, the links between the public and the private sector.

In the Dutch case, these links were close: the site was developed jointly. In Houston, this was rather the opposite, since the development was solely carried out by the developer, and the city was only involved as the enforcer of its own code of ordinances. In Bristol, the city takes an intermediary position. These positions are not exclusively and specifically related to these cases, but reflect a more general pattern in each country. This affects transaction costs[3].

## Attitudes towards transaction costs

A more specific, transaction-cost related, element of the relationship between public and private, is the attitude towards (the incidence of) transaction costs. There are different perceptions and attitudes towards transaction costs and how to reduce them. Transaction-cost economics implicitly assumes actors who strive to reduce transaction costs. But one of the reasons for the occurrence and size of transaction costs is, possibly, transaction-cost awareness, or a lack thereof. Looking at the cases, there seem to be different degrees of awareness. The cases also differ in the way local governments think and deal with the transaction costs borne by private developers. Efficiency and customer service play a bigger role in Houston than in the city of Nijmegen. The three cities and the three countries show differences in their attitude towards and treatment of transaction costs (see Chapter 8).

## Legal styles: flexibility, certainty and accountability

The last element of the institutional context that gets attention in Chapter 8, is the legal style (see also Newman & Thornley, 1996; Booth, 1996), which is closely related to the meso-level institutions – public and private law rules with regard to land use and exchange – as I defined then in Chapter 3 and discussed them in the subsequent case chapters.

The legal style in the case studies largely follows the national legal styles. This has a consequence for transaction costs. In Houston, legal certainty is very high, since all the rules are known in advance and are the same for nearly every location. The English case is the opposite, since there are no legally binding conditions that are known in

---

[3] Dimension one and two – that is, the quest for control and the relationship between public and private – have in similar forms been the subject of comparisons between planning cultures (see, e.g. Sanyal, 2005). Planning cultures can be defined as: '[...] the collective ethos and dominant attitudes of planners regarding the appropriate role of the state, market forces, and civil society in influencing social outcomes' (Sanyal, 2005, p. XXI). But also urban regime research (see e.g. Kantor *et al.*, 1997) makes comparisons that focus on the power balance in coalitions between the public and the private sector. The relationship between these kinds of research and transaction costs will be made in Chapter 8.

advance. In the Netherlands, there is more legal certainty than in England, but less than in Houston. The situation for accountability is different. Because the city of Houston is involved in specific land-use decisions to only a limited extent, it cannot account for the decisions made about the kind of use to which the land is put. Accountability to third parties is 'decentralised' to the landowners. The Dutch municipalities are at the other extreme, whereas the English cites are once again somewhere in between. This has a major effect not only on the size, but also on the way, transaction costs are distributed. The legal style – together with the other three categories – in relation to transaction costs, will be elaborated upon in more detail in Chapter 8.

# References

Adams, D., Disberry, A., Hutchison, N. & Munjoma, T. (2002) Land policy and urban renaissance: the impact of ownership constraints in four British cities. *Planning Theory and Practice* **3**(2): 195–217.

Booth, P. (1996) *Controlling Development. Certainty and Discretion in Europe, the USA and Hong Kong.* UCL Press, London.

Buitelaar, E., Mertens, H., Needham, B. & De Kam, G. (2006) *Sturend Vermogen En Woningbouw: Een Onderzoek Naar Het Vermogen Van Gemeenten Om Te Sturen Bij De Ontwikkeling Van Woningbouwlocaties.* DGW/NETHUR, Den Haag/Utrecht.

Friedmann, J. (2003) Why do planning theory? *Planning Theory* **2**(1): 7–10.

Kantor, P., Savitch, H. V. & Vicari Haddock, S. (1997) The political economy of urban regimes: a comparative perspective. *Urban Affairs Review* **32**(3): 348–77.

Newman, P. & Thornley, A. (1996) *Urban Planning in Europe: International Competition, National Systems & Planning Projects.* Routledge, London/New York.

Sanyal, B. (ed.) (2005) *Comparative Planning Cultures.* Routledge, New York.

Van Gunsteren, H. R. (1976) *The Quest for Control. A Critique of the Rational–Central-Rule Approach in Public Affairs.* John Wiley & Sons, London.

Webster, C. J. (2005) The new institutional economics and the evolution of modern urban planning. *Town Planning Review* **76**(4): 455–84.

Williamson, O. E. (1996) *The Mechanisms of Governance.* Oxford University Press, New York.

Wood, A. M. (2004) Domesticating urban theory? US concepts, British cities and the limits of cross-national applications. *Urban Studies* **41**(11): 2103–18.

# 8

# Transaction Costs and the Institutional Context

Chapter 7 concluded with four dimensions of social structure that might best explain the emergence, size and distribution of transaction costs that have been observed in the three case studies. These dimensions are elaborated upon in this chapter. Although they are analytically distinguished, they are in practice closely intertwined. In their turn they are related to and embedded in other structural levels, such as doctrines about the role of the state in general or other deeply rooted social values. It is beyond the scope of this book to analyse all of those systematically. When necessary and appropriate, reference will be made to these social structures. The analysis in this chapter is based on findings from the three case studies, additional empirical research and literature in the planning field and related areas.

## The quest for control over development

There is a clear link between the level of control that public authorities want to exercise and the transaction costs that result from it. In the Houston case, the city restricted itself to enforcing its own ordinances, whereas the city of Nijmegen was actively involved in the development from the very beginning, seeking as much control over the final output as possible. This approach requires much more input from the local bureaucracy. In addition, it significantly extends the development process, since more negotiation and deliberation between the developer and the local authority is needed.

The emphasis on control is related to the unit of analysis: the transaction. In Chapter 2, I defined the transaction – following John Commons – as a *legal action to increase (or take) control over property rights.* What this research has shown is that not every authority has the same ambition or desire to *control.* It is not only the general wish to control, but also the level of detail in which local authorities want control that might differ between government agencies. Therefore, the quest for control has been divided into two dimensions: the wish to control and the level of detail at which control is exercised (see Figure 8.1).

If we look at Figure 8.1, the Dutch case could be situated somewhere around the letter A, because the city wanted to be in control, and wanted to be in control at a high level of detail. In the Houstonian case, the city quite clearly maintains more distance and has less desire to regulate land use. However, when it does want to take control, like in flood plain management or subdivision reviews, it does so at a similar level of detail as the city of Nijmegen did at the Marialaan. It can therefore be placed around C. Wapping Wharf has a more intermediary position. The wish to control is higher than in Houston. But because of the English reactionary, instead of anticipatory, development control system (despite the changes that have been made, since the adoption

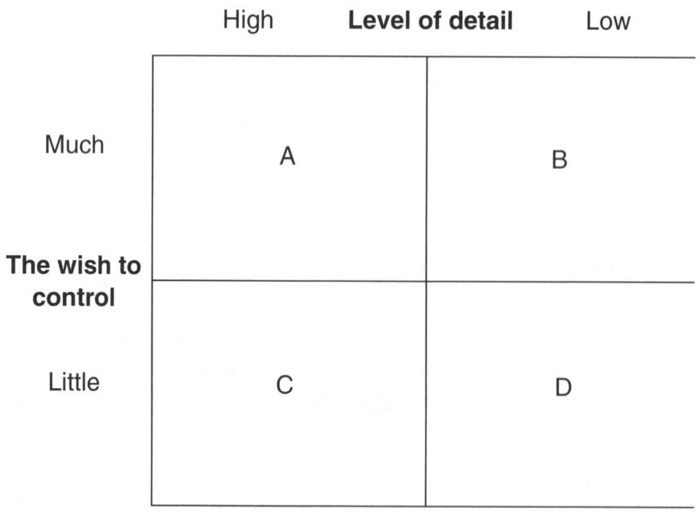

Figure 8.1  The quest for control.

of the Planning and Compensation Act 1991 and the Planning and Compulsory Purchase Act 2004, to make it a more plan-led system), it is lower than in the Dutch case. The level of detail, however, is quite similar (that is, high) as that in the other situations (see e.g. Allmendinger & Ball, 2006). Therefore, it must be positioned somewhere between A and C. It must be noted that this is purely an analytical and indicative distinction that is not applicable one-to-one.

The position of each case in the matrix is to some extent representative for its country. There seems to be a greater quest for control over spatial development in the Netherlands than in England and Houston. The qualification of Nadin *et al.* (1997) of the nature of planning traditions illustrates this nicely. They argue that the Dutch system is associated with a comprehensive integrated approach. Faludi argues that the wish to create order in the Dutch landscape is an important feature of the planning culture (Faludi & Van Der Valk, 1994; Faludi, 2005). He also argues (2005) that the Netherlands has a 'soft spot for planning'. A nice illustration of this, related to transaction costs, is given by Hajer *et al.* (2006), who say that they know no other country that spends hundreds of millions of Euros on stimulating 'innovative land use' and 'transition management'. But it needs to be said that the wish to control is not the same as having control, since the amount of control exercised has begun to come under pressure from factors such as increased competition in planning, globalisation, shifts within the public sector and so on (Hajer *et al.* 2006).

Houston, as mentioned before, clearly does not have such a planning culture. There is a limited wish to control development. The city sees itself primarily as a facilitator, catalyst and enabler of growth and development, rather than an actor that wants to steer development in a certain direction. Recently there have been several initiatives by the city to initiate development (like a tax increment reinvestment zone). In addition, there are general and well-known ways of facilitating development, such as the development of roads, water supply and waste-water treatment plants ahead of new developments. There are obviously restrictions on land use, such as subdivision and building regulations, but they are not location-specific, as in the case of land-use plans and zoning, and hence do not have discriminatory effects. They are general and relate to every development on every location. Houston does not plan ahead in terms of strategic and land use plans; it hardly develops land itself like Dutch municipalities do, and it hardly gets involved in making sure that incompatible land uses are not located next to each other.

This latter element has been the key feature of the English system for a long time. Nadin *et al.* (1997) qualify the English planning tradition as one of 'land use management', meaning that government intervention does not go further than keeping incompatible land uses, like housing and heavy industry, apart. This was, for instance, clearly stated in the HMSO (1985) white paper *Lifting the burden*, which recommended that councils confine themselves to preventing negative externalities and not get involved in determining which design is acceptable. It was the development industry's role to come up with the initiatives. One result is that transaction costs that are made by the local government occur at a different stage in England than in the Netherlands. In Holland, planning is more forward-looking than in England. This leads to more transaction costs being made in earlier stages of the process in a Dutch development scheme.

Related to this, is the difference in the way local authorities are involved in land development. Because of their ambition to control, Dutch local authorities are often active land developers. Therefore, compulsory purchase in the Netherlands is used more often than in England[1]. In 1999, the UK Urban Task Force stated that ownership constraints were a major impediment to urban regeneration (Cullingworth & Nadin, 2006). One of its observations was that there was a widespread reluctance among local authorities to use compulsory purchase because of the bureaucratic nature of the process, the complexity of its legal procedures, the lack of necessary skills and the inadequacy of compensation arrangements (Adams *et al.*, 2002). The lack of skills is the result of more market-oriented approaches that developed in the 1980s when compulsory purchase fell into disuse. In the 1950s and 1960s it was widely used.

This shows that practices and cultural elements are never static, and this also holds true for the future. If the newly defined ambitions in the new English planning act and the planning policy statements are implemented at the local level, forward planning, creating sustainable communities and a more active involvement in the implementation of plans will get a more prominent role in England. Recently the modifier 'spatial' (instead of town and country, or land use) has become

---

[1] A survey among 294 local planning authorities showed that 243 of them did not use compulsory purchase between mid-1992 and mid-1992 (Adams *et al.*, 2001).

fashionable in England, indicating a shift towards a more comprehensive, integrated and proactive approach to planning that goes beyond adjusting and regulating land uses[2]. Especially since the Labour government came to power in 1997, the need was felt for government agencies to become more active and ambitious with regard to spatial development, in order to deliver goals such as sustainability, economic growth (especially in the north of England and the Midlands) and increased housing production. Planning Policy Statement 1 now says that planning:

> '... goes beyond traditional land use planning to bring together and integrate policies for the development and use of land with other policies and programmes which influence the nature of places and how they function.'

The government has also emphasised the importance of a good design for creating sustainable communities.

> 'This relates to: the design of, and materials used in, individual buildings as well as the overall pattern of development, including building densities, car parking and street layouts.'
>
> (Audit Commission, 2006b, p. 11)

One could say that the ambition to control spatial development is increasing. The report by the Audit Commission, referred to earlier, clearly links transaction costs and the quest for control, as the title of the report indicates: *The Planning System: Matching Expectations and Capacity* (Audit Commission, 2006b). The expectations, and the quest for control, are rising, while the capacity – both qualitatively and quantitatively – is lagging. There are too few people with the appropriate skills to fill the new roles – at the moment of writing, there were 18000 planning positions in England, of which 4000 were vacant (interview with Eamon Mythen). More transaction costs need to be incurred to achieve the new ambitions (but also to achieve old ambitions). If we compare the number of people working in 'planning' in the Netherlands to the number in some English cities we see a big

---

[2] To give an example, the University of the West of England (in Bristol) has set up a Master's course in spatial planning financed by the ODPM, which is based for a large part on ideas on planning, and especially integration, that have emerged in countries in continental Europe like the Netherlands.

difference in the number of officers (see Appendix B), both absolute and related to the number of inhabitants. The Audit Commission therefore suggests making more use of private consultants, for work where local authorities have insufficient expertise and not enough capacity. Consultancy companies are mainly employed by the development industry and not so much by the public sector, although this seems to be changing (Audit Commission, 2006b, pp. 35–36). The use of consultants by municipalities in the Netherlands is much more widespread (Askew & Hartogs, 2005). In England, more transaction costs (that is, more staff) will have to be made to meet the goals and the expectations.

This poses not only serious challenges in quantitative terms – that is, the transaction costs – but also for the planning culture. People working in development control are used to imposing conditions and separating land uses. But:

> 'As councils move away from narrow land use planning, planners increasingly interact with other professionals in order to plan for the interrelationships that happen in mixed communities. This poses challenges for established planners.'
>
> (Audit Commission, 2006b)

People need to be trained more in land policy (for example compulsory purchase and valuation), design skills and communicative skills. Local planning authorities will also have to overcome the rather negative image that has evolved. A job in development control is generally valued lower than one in the private sector (see also, Allmendinger & Ball, 2006). One reason for that is people's perception of the planning system:

> 'The planning system in local government has suffered from many years of being portrayed as the problem rather than the solution.'
>
> (Burning & Glasson, 2004)

## Relationship between public and private sector

Before the development of the Marialaan entered the formal *bestemmingsplan* procedure, numerous meetings were held, both between municipal departments and between the municipality and the developer. It took five years before an agreement was reached and the plans were made definite. Although this might seem exceptionally long for out-siders, it is fairly common in the Netherlands that public and private parties incur high transaction costs on deliberation and negotiation. Transaction costs are subordinate to this institutionalised practice in which building trust is essential. Even the municipality of Breda, a city with an explicit business-like attitude, admits that it has sometimes difficulty refraining from open and non-committal discussions with developers in the early stages of the development process, which give rise to (in their view) unnecessary transaction costs. Trust can reduce transaction costs, but unconditional trust can lead to uncertainties and a lack of progress (Van Ark, 2005), and hence more transaction costs, since no need is felt to confirm decisions by formalising them. At the Marialaan, this was also the case, for it took several years before the municipality and the developer decided that the process needed to accelerate and that agreements had to be formalised.

This Dutch practice in which private parties and public authorities closely cooperate with each other is not limited to spatial planning, but is common in many areas of government regulation. Social security issues have (until recently) been resolved by close cooperation between the government, employers' associations and labour associations. This has become famous as the 'Dutch miracle', as opposed to the 'Dutch disease' that was used to term the severe problems Holland had with social-economic issues in the 1970s. The collaborative, or corporatist, model is generally referred to as the *Poldermodel*. It must be noted that this has come under criticism since the beginning of this millennium which has led to a gradual decline of the confidence in the model.

In England there is a much more distant and less intimate relation-ship in general between public and private parties. Pre-application meetings – also called front-loading – between local officers and devel-opers are an emerging phenomenon, but are still by no means compa-rable to the way Dutch municipalities and developers cooperate before the submission of the planning application. Nor are the planning agreements – following section 106 of the Town and Country Planning Act 1990 – similar to the development and intention agreement that the city of Nijmegen and the developer signed. A planning agreement contains actions that the developer has to take to compensate the community for the development. It can be a unilateral undertaking, meaning that the developer can impose planning obligations on himself to enhance his chances for getting a planning permission. In the other situation, when both the local planning authority and the developer sign the 'agreement', it is not voluntarily entered into. To use Scharpf's words, it is 'bargaining under the shadow of law' (Scharpf, 1997). The agreements hardly ever contain obligations for the local authority, in contrast to many of the agreements Dutch municipalities sign. Intimacy between developers and local authorities can have positive effects for transaction costs, for trust can prevent deadlocks, but it can also raise transaction costs, by removing an incentive to proceed quickly. The latter is often the case in the Netherlands.

The relationship in Houston between the city of Houston and the business elite is very close. Moreover, it is one of the key features and forces behind Houston's economic development (Feagin, 1988). With regard to spatial development, the city plays an important role. One of the major catalysts for urban development is infrastructure. Subsidising and developing major infrastructure projects, like roads, light rail, the extension of the airport and developments in the maritime port have been the main pillars of the city development strategy to facilitate urban development and economic growth (see also, Neuman, 2003b). However, when it comes to development control – that is, the 'nitty gritty' of planning practice – the city refrains from getting involved too much in decisions about how the land should be used. The municipality merely acts as an enforcer of the Code of Ordinances. This role limits the involvement of the City of Houston and the transaction costs it bears.

## Attitudes towards transaction costs

The attitudes towards transaction costs, especially from public agencies, are a particular aspect of the relationship between the public and the private sector. We will now look into this in more detail for each country separately.

### Netherlands

From the case studies, general observations on the three countries and secondary literature (e.g. Nadin *et al.*, 1997; Sanyal, 2005), we could conclude that Dutch local authorities are more actively involved in the development process than their equivalents in the other two countries. This observation is also supported if we look at the number of people involved in planning (see Appendix B).

This big involvement has consequences for the transaction costs that are directly related to a project, and this makes it interesting to look into it in more detail. To do this, I have looked at several cities (particularly Nijmegen, Breda and Den Haag). How do these municipalities deal with transaction costs, how do they keep them under control and how do they cover their expenses? These questions cannot be answered in general terms, since there are very few national and general rules for transaction costs. There are similarities, but also many differences, in the way local authorities deal with them.

In Chapter 4, it was mentioned that Dutch municipalities, when drawing up a land servicing account, include a certain percentage of the costs of (physically) preparing the land for housing to cover their own administrative costs. This norm is called VTA, – although there are many equivalents – which stands for preparation, supervision and administration. This has become common practice for land development in general. Initially, this norm was set by the national government in the 1960s and 1970s, between 19 and 22%[3]. The assumption was that 12 to 15% was needed for all the costs related to the land servicing works (but not the production costs of the works themselves) and that 7% was needed for related research, such as investigations of soil contamination. Many municipalities used this (and some still do) for many decades. However, it is now extended to cover other costs as well, like the costs of financial experts, project managers, municipal designers and so forth (see Chapter 4 for a more complete overview for the city of Nijmegen). It must be noted, however, that the activities included in the VTA costs vary significantly between municipalities. Nijmegen and Breda, for instance, include every activity related to the project, up to approval of the *bestemmingsplan* by the province. Many other municipalities do not include the formal procedures (see e.g. Van Hoek, 2004).

These VTA percentages, however, do not necessarily reflect the real costs that will be or have been made. First, they are an estimation of the costs. During the process the financial experts, based on information from planning and control, can monitor whether the reservation

---

[3] The reason that the national government did this, was because it subsidized land for social housing. It wanted to keep the land prices under control. The more land municipalities gave out for social housing, the more subsidies they would get from the national government. To keep the land prices, and therewith the subsidies under control, the national government made norms for each cost item, so also for VTA.

must be adjusted. In practice, however, hardly any municipality calculates after the project whether the estimation was correct; it is too complex and costly. In addition, VTA is a percentage of the land servicing works, while many of the activities that are regarded as part of the VTA, like project management, urban design and even strategic spatial policy, have very little to do with these works. Another difficulty is that VTA is a percentage of the costs of the physical preparation of a site. In a project with a lot of engineering works (like bridges, roads and railways) and high costs related to that, the VTA amount, which is based on a percentage of those costs, could be low while the absolute process costs can be quite high.

From the literature (Nijland, 2005; Van Hoek, 2004) and the interviews, we can see an increase in the VTA costs. Many local authorities now use a percentage that is above 22% (depending on the type of project), usually somewhere between 25 and 30%. There are various explanations as to why these costs have risen. First, projects have become more complex, for many reasons. One is that local authorities do not have the land monopoly they used to have: developers have acquired much land. In addition, in 1995 the housing associations were cut loose from national subsidies, which forced them to become more active developers to cover the costs of letting social houses. These two developments have led to a 'busier' land market, which has forced municipalities to cooperate more with other actors (for instance in public–private partnerships). This increases the transaction costs. There is also an increase in the number of rules and regulations, especially in the environmental field, not the least due to an increase of European rules. The last important element is the gradual shift from greenfield development to the redevelopment of city centres, and pre- and early post-war housing areas. Redevelopment projects are generally more complex and transaction-cost consuming than greenfield sites.

A second reason for the increased VTA costs is the increase in the number of activities that are included in it and an increase in the wages of the various departments that bear on the individual land servicing accounts. There are two reasons. Project-based working has been introduced in many municipalities, which means that the project managers and the land development department have become principals, and the other departments have become agents. In addition, municipalities and their departments have to deal with budget cutbacks, so they try to cover as much expenditure as possible by land development projects.

In Nijmegen, the (internal) costs of a man hour have been increased by nearly 10% each year in the last couple of years, leading to the situation where the costs of internal labour are no longer significantly lower than those of external consultants. The city of Breda argues that the internal costs of labour in some departments (like geo-information) are even higher than those externally. One reason is that overheads are being charged. It depends on the project managers and, politically, on the municipal councils, to what extent this is allowed. A major disadvantage of this practice is that the VTA could reduce the amount of money available for other, more substantial issues in urban development projects.

The third reason is that the transaction costs have been made more explicit and transparent in some cities, because of the project-based way of working. Also, due to the earlier mentioned cutbacks, departments try to cover as many of their departmental costs – overheads as well – by land development. As a result, urban development costs have become more clear and explicit. The VTAs that are now often charged are in line with research that was carried out in 1981 by a consultant commissioned by the Ministry for spatial planning (VROM). This calculated that the percentage, instead of the generally used 19 and 22 %, should be around 37% for small (fewer than 500 units) projects and 30% for bigger projects (interview with Gerrit Verkerk).

Dutch municipalities are, in general, not very good at controlling the (rise of) transaction costs. The design and the financial side are often not well connected (Vrom-Raad, 2004). One way of dealing with the rise in transaction costs is by reserving a bigger percentage (25 to 30%) than before (19 to 22%) on the land servicing account. The city of Breda tries to avoid this, because increasing the percentage does not reduce the costs, it simply acknowledges higher costs. Breda sticks to the 22% that has been used since the 1960s and 1970s, and tries the keep the real VTA costs within that percentage. When there are unanticipated costs, the budget is sometimes increased – if the rise in costs is motivated properly – but this is not a default mechanism. The development department of the city divides the percentage among the various activities (that is, the departments that carry out those activities), based on standard data and percentages, which gives an indication of what the various departments can spend. Then the departments have to make a proposal about what they can do, in how much time and with how much money. This gives the development department insight in what to expect, when and for how much and provides a tool to control the costs and the length of the process. However, this requires a different attitude, and even a different culture, in public organisations. The city of Breda has been working with this approach for around 20 years and it has taken many years for people to get used to it. One can design new management structures but the 'soft infrastructure' (or the informal institutions) need to be in place as well. The Hague started this way of working a few years ago, but it has not succeeded in implementing and – more important – sticking to it entirely[4]. The Hague is probably no exception.

In the Netherlands, there can be various ways of recouping the transaction costs made by the municipality. When the municipality owns the land and develops it, transaction costs can be recouped if the development gain is big enough. Currently, a new act is being prepared that will make it easier for local authorities to recoup plan costs along the lines of public law (if it does not own the land). It could be that this will take away an incentive to speed up the process and to keep the costs of the process low. Municipalities could take a relaxed attitude, knowing that they can receive a certain sum for their efforts, irrespective of these efforts. Developers often need the municipalities to change the land use plan, or they need public space for building land. When development is carried out by the municipality itself, interest rates provide an incentive to make sure that there are no unnecessary delays.

Beside these practices, there are the fees to recoup the costs of the formal development control procedure. Municipalities determine the size of the fees (although they should not comprise more than 100% of the real costs), and the city of Nijmegen proves to be quite successful in optimising its benefits from them, since these are higher than the real costs of processing the planning applications (see Chapter 4). Until now, there has been little resistance from the development industry against having to pay municipalities for transaction costs over which they – the developers – have no control. As long as there are profits in abundance, developers accept the recovery of transaction costs by municipalities. Moreover, all municipalities do it, so there is no point

---

[4] What sometimes happens is that different departments put costs on a project, which the project manager is not able to check to see whether these were necessary and whether they were actually spent. With clear tasks, assignments and agreements, managing accounts becomes easier.

in shopping around. The new land management act – that was in preparation at the moment of writing – will most likely discipline this practice.

## England

Unlike the Netherlands, in England the initiatives to manage transaction cost come primarily from central government, and are related to development control. In addition, England has, as one of the interviewees phrased it, an 'auditing culture', meaning that performance of local authorities is measured and made transparent (that is, through naming and shaming), by the central government.

One of the major goals of central government with regard to the planning system is speeding up the planning process, since it is assumed that this will improve the economic competitiveness of the whole country (Audit Commission, 2006b). Speed is seen as the key issue for delivering a higher quality of planning services. The time taken to determine planning applications is one of the indicators for the Audit Commission[5] to assess overall performance of local authorities. The audit commission says about Bristol:

> 'The council needs to achieve value for money more consistently, and routinely make the link between the cost of the service, its performance and public satisfaction.'    (Audit Commission, 2006a)

On the basis of this assessment local authorities are categorized, which affects the amount of funding they get from central government.

The bigger developments, called 'major decisions', are supposed to be decided within 13 weeks, while 'minor' and 'other' should be decided in 8 weeks. If one looks at the performance of local planning authorities on major decisions, we can see – not surprisingly – that the smaller authorities with fewer applications perform best[6]. The top 5 of

---

[5] The Audit Commission is an independent statutory body responsible for assessing and reporting on the performance of local authorities. It describes itself as an agency that ensures that '[...] public money is spent economically, efficiently, and effectively, to achieve high quality local services for the public'.

[6] These are data for district councils, London Boroughs, unitary authorities and national park authorities. They can be found on the ODPM website: www.odpm.gov.uk.

the ODPM rank decides all its major decisions within 13 weeks; but they had no major decisions. Bristol is ranked number 240 (out of a total of 362 local planning authorities), with 182 decisions made, of which 51% were decided within 13 weeks. This rank is used for rewarding local planning authorities that perform according to or above the standards set. The size of the grant – Planning Delivery Grant (PDG) – is determined on the basis of the performance rank of the local planning authority and its workload[7]. To give an example, for the major decisions: when a local planning authority decides between 60% and 65% of its decisions within 13 weeks, it will get £33 333 if it makes 20 or fewer decisions, £50 000 between 20 and 39 decisions, £66 667 between 40 and 99 decisions, and £100 000 for 100 decisions or more, per year (ODPM, 2005b). The other two categories for major decisions are '65 and 70' and 70+. The 'minor' and 'other' decisions have other (higher) percentages, related to different (higher) numbers of decisions to meet.

According to the Audit Commission and the ODPM, these incentive structures have led in many cases to councils performing better, like the London boroughs and many rural districts, which have streamlined their organisational structure and processes. Between 2003 and 2005, 160 local planning authorities had improved their performance (ODPM, 2005a). In addition, it is claimed that the incentives have changed the culture in many local authorities towards more performance orientated cultures (ODPM, 2005c), especially with regard to transaction costs. A positive effect is also that authorities who were able to increase their grant tend to spend it on forward (or strategic) planning alongside development control (ODPM, 2005a).

However, the grant system has also led to more 'unwanted', or at least unplanned, effects[8] that give rise to transaction costs. First, there has been a rise in the number of refusals of planning permissions (Audit Commission, 2006b); in 2004 there was an increase of 13.7% on 2005

---

[7] There are not only quantitative criteria with regard to development control (that is, speed), but also quantitative and qualitative criteria for policy-making as well.

[8] The ODPM (in an interview) argues that in many cases it is good that applications are refused under the pressure of the performance systems. Earlier, planning officers were probably more inclined to process applications that contained very little detail and provided very little information. Now they refuse it more easily, which can be seen as an improvement of efficiency.

(ODPM, 2005c)[9]. In addition, the better performing authorities (in terms of decision time) have marginally higher refusal rates (ODPM, 2004). Most likely as a result of the increase in refusals (Arup, 2004), there is a growing number of appeals received and handled by the Planning Inspectorate; from 2001 till 2005 the number increased every year from 16 737 to 23 161 appeals per year, an increase of 38% (Planning Inspectorate, 2005). Developers often go to an appeal if permission is refused. Another way to meet the target is to try to persuade the developer to withdraw his application if it does not meet the requirements. There has been a rise in withdrawals of 16.4% between 2003 and 2004. Notwithstanding the rise in the number of refusals, withdrawals and appeals, only few authorities felt that the quality was being compromised by the increased speed in development control (ODPM, 2005a).

Yet another practice that has emerged, and one that is welcomed by the central government, is the use of pre-applications. The pre-application stage is a more informal stage that is not exposed in the performance rankings. It is used by local authorities to communicate their requirements to the developers and make suggestions for change, so that the formal application process runs more smoothly. It is used by developers to obtain advice and to assess the likelihood of getting planning permission and to know the kind of planning conditions and obligations that might be imposed. Many stakeholders are enthusiastic about this new practice, since it can save time and money (that is, transaction costs) in later stages. Private developers are even willing to pay for it, as long as they meet people at the appropriate level to give a helpful response (Audit Commission 2006b, pp. 54–55).

The Audit Commission itself questions whether the emphasis on speed is always useful. For the major applications, certainty of the time scale is often more important than speed, something which has also been noted with regard to projects in the Netherlands (De Bruijn *et al.*, 1996). Due to the increase in agencies involved and the increased complexity, a standard performance measure for major decisions is less appropriate than for small-scale projects (see also Allmendinger & Ball, 2006). Nevertheless, the general opinion is that development

---

[9] However, it remains subject to debate whether the emphasis on speed is responsible for the increase in refusals. The ODPM is not so sure about this (2005a). But the Audit Commission (2006b) held many interviews in which this was repeatedly argued.

control has become more efficient and absorbs fewer transaction costs. It should be noted that some of these gains are reduced by some of the side effects that have been mentioned.

A major difference with the Netherlands is that the fees of the local planning authorities are by no means sufficient to cover the costs of running the planning system. At the moment of writing, an accountant's office was carrying out national research to investigate the relationship between the real costs to the planning authorities of the planning process, and the fees charged. The absolute maximum fee at this moment for any kind of residential development is £50 000. Since applying for building regulations is separate from development control, there is a different and additional fee for building permissions.

As a result of the PDG, the emphasis now put on pre-application discussions between developers and local authorities has led to tensions, since authorities do not want to use the formal determination time for extensive discussions and negotiations. For that reason, central government allows local authorities to charge fees for pre-application. This 'front-loading', implies that more of the decision-making (and hence transaction costs) takes place in the earlier stages of the development process. The size of the fees for pre-applications is at the discretion of the local planning authority. In a recent report by the ODPM, it was noted that, from a sample it held at that moment, no local authority has charged anything for the pre-application stage (ODPM, 2005c). This is consistent with what the interviewees told me.

### Houston

Government regulation is an issue in every country, no matter how (favourably) that country compares to others. Nationwide research on subdivision regulations (Seidel, 1978; Ben-Joseph, 2003) shows that in the US also, there is debate on land use regulations in relation to transaction costs. Ben-Joseph says:

> 'With our survey indicating a steady increase over the last 25 years in the average time it takes to receive subdivision approval the increase in costs has undoubtedly been transferred to the consumer.'[10]
>
> (Ben-Joseph, 2003, p. 15)

---

[10] It should be noted that when a residual price model is applied (see, e.g. Needham, 1992), it is not the costs that determine the price. The costs only influence the size and the distribution of the margins in the building chain.

Another interesting quotation in the light of transaction costs is that of the Urban Land Institute:

'American developers of housing must deal with an expanding array of regulations at every level of government. Unreasonable regulations on development inevitably inflate paperwork required for a project and intensify the complexity of data, analysis, and review procedures for both pubic and private sector. Ultimately, the delay caused by the regulatory maze produces higher cost housing through holding costs, increased expenses due to risk, uncertainty, overhead, and inflated cost of labour and materials, and other more hidden costs.' (Ben-Joseph, 2003, p. 17)

Both surveys report many delays in the approval process, though the reasons for delay vary. Almost all public officials point to the developers and argue that they provide inadequate information and change their plans. However, there are also officials that say that the coordination between different agencies and commissions and the inefficient management of the approval process can be blamed for the delays. Despite all these criticisms, it seems as if development control, especially in Houston, is less costly and time-consuming than in the English and Dutch cases.

Houston has much autonomy – compared to the other cases – in deciding how to handle transaction costs. Although Houston seems to compare favourably in terms of transaction costs (also when looking at Appendix B), especially to Dutch cities, there are also complaints about the regulations. For that reason, the mayor of Houston installed a taskforce – the mayor's building permit task force – to investigate the practice of public reviews of the development process. The taskforce reported in 2004 (The Mayor's Building Permit Task Force, 2004) that although Houston compares well with other cities in the US[11], in terms of the effectiveness and quality of customer services, it should also be noted that there are many process inefficiencies and that the city's bureaucracy is complex.

After this report, a steering committee was appointed with the task of implementing the report's proposals. The report contains some interesting findings about transaction costs that are caused by the creation

---

[11] In addition, one of the interviewees noted that companies that develop nationally – like Wall Mart – are enthusiastic about the speed of plan review in Houston.

and the use of the user rights regime. It notes that, although it may sound paradoxical for a city that is called the *Free Enterprise City* (Feagin, 1988), Houston's plan review process is 'far more extensive' than many other major cities (which contradicts one of the central conclusions that Houston compares favourably with other cities). Various workshops were held with both suppliers (city officials and staff) and users (professionals from Houston's real estate development community) of the permitting services. In a survey that was held among the participants, 60% said it was 'hard or very hard' to secure the necessary site development approvals (like platting, utilities, easements, flood plain and related requirements). 52% of them said the plan review process was 'hard or very hard' compared to other cities. One common factor mentioned in the plan review process that leads to inefficiencies, is the communication between plan reviewers and applicants. This is especially the case for first time applicants who are not familiar with the process and do not exactly know which requirements they have to meet and which steps they have to go through. This, together with the relatively short time frame for plan reviews (between 45 and 90 days on average), are factors behind rejections and sometimes inefficiencies.

The validity of this report, however, is questionable. As one of the interviewees from the City of Houston said: 'No attempts have been made to make the survey statistically reliable'. But what the report at least shows is the city's intention to reduce transaction costs, not only for itself but also for the applicant. The transaction-cost awareness seems to be much higher in Houston than in the English, and especially the Dutch, cities. Reducing transaction costs for developers and inhabitants is explicitly seen as a tool to attract investment in the context of territorial competition. There are all sorts of initiatives aimed at reducing transaction costs for applicants. Two of them – the building permit taskforce and the steering committee – have already been mentioned. Another is the Neighborhood Technical Assistance Center, established by the city, which helps and facilitates communities to set up and enforce restrictive covenants. In addition, there is the city's Deed Restrictions Pro Bono Program, in collaboration with the Houston Bar Association and the Houston Volunteer Lawyer's Program (HVLP), to provide free legal assistance for people on low incomes who want to create or modify their restrictive covenants. The City of Houston is not only looking for ways to cut its own costs, but it also pays attention to how transaction costs might affect development and private initiatives. In Houston, the City wants to be competitive on transaction costs by providing short 'customer' time. The word 'customer' already indicates how it wants to deal with applicants. This orientation on 'customers' and the wish to reduce transaction costs for them seems much more pronounced in Houston than in Bristol and Nijmegen.

Although projects can have lower transaction costs in Houston, compared to Nijmegen and Bristol, it does not mean that the costs of regulating spatial development in the city are lower. In the absence of zoning, and often in the presence of fear, people decide to enter into restrictive covenants to govern neighbourhoods. This development is widespread throughout the US (Mckenzie, 2003). In 2006, the US had 286 000 'association-governed communities' that include homeowners associations, condominiums, cooperatives and other planned communities. These communities comprise 23.1 million housing units occupied by 57 million Americans (www.caionline.org). The deed restricted neighbourhoods often have far greater levels of micro-regulation (Mckenzie, 2003). There are many websites and discussion forums in the US that are used by people to complain about the restrictiveness of some of these community or homeowners' associations. However, there is an increasing number of people who want to live in deed restricted estates. When an estate is developed, the developer often decides to impose deed restrictions to the plat that run with the land. These are mainly designed to prevent negative externalities. In this way, each single landowner does not have to enter into bilateral arrangements with neighbours to achieve the same result. This joining up in housing associations or residential clubs thus reduces transaction costs. Needham (2006b) argues that the transaction costs of private law should not be under estimated; in the US there ten times more advocates per head of the population than there are in the Netherlands.

Secondly, there are consequences of the fact that the City of Houston is not accountable for the decision to develop. When there is an objection from an adjacent plot owner, he has to direct his attention and objections to the developer directly. This can lead to serious conflicts and even cancellation of projects. An interesting example is Near Rice University (the self-declared 'Harvard of the South') where a developer called off the development of a high-rise condominium development (Houston Chronicle, 2005), because of objections by the neighbourhood.

For that reason, developers are not necessarily against transaction costs, if they reduce the costs incurred in later stages.

There are some clear differences in the way the municipalities in each country deal with transaction costs. In England, central government has introduced performance management, planning delivery grants and so on; all initiatives to reduce transactions costs. There is not a great deal of variation in the way local authorities can manage their performance in terms of transaction costs. This is different in the Netherlands and even more so in the US. But what is also different is the attitude towards the incidence of transaction costs. What the performance measures in England and the Netherlands have in common is the priority for reducing transaction costs for the public authorities themselves, whereas the city Houston is also looking explicitly at the costs that applicants bear as a result of public rules.

This raises the question of to what extent the developer should pay for public services, most notably development control? An argument that is quite often used is that it is in the interest of the developer that the planning services are offered, for that makes development possible. But the developer is often not the only one who benefits from the result of the development process. Therefore, in England there is some opposition from the development industry against ideas from central government about 'full cost recovery' (CBI, 2005). A neighbourhood and even a whole city could benefit from certain (re)developments. Local authorities often have their own particular wishes. Development control is not only used to facilitate and enable development (which could possibly justify payment by a developer), but also, as the term indicates, to exercise control over development. So when should developers be held accountable for the transaction costs of public planning? It is striking that Dutch developers accept the demands that they pay 100% of the municipality's development costs. In England also, some developers prefer to pay part of the transaction costs if this increases certainty and reduces risks. Solicitors employed by the local planning authority to draw up the section 106 agreements are sometimes paid by the developers to keep the process going.

As we saw especially in the Houston case, developers sometimes willingly accept transaction costs, especially the (interest) costs of a longer development process, if they expect the benefits of waiting – that is, higher house prices – to exceed the costs. Therefore there is ambivalence toward the costs of using user rights regimes. They are seen as barriers, inevitabilities and sometimes as opportunities.

## Legal styles: flexibility, certainty and accountability

Every system of development control is different, but there is one major theme that runs through all the systems. Each tries to find a balance between flexibility and certainty in decision making (Allmendinger & Ball, 2006). The way the balance is established differs in every country. The English system has become known as a discretionary system, which means that the plan is indicative and not legally binding, and the planning decision is determined on its merits, taking into account various 'material considerations'. For the transaction costs related to the user rights regime, this means that most are made and borne both by the developer and by the municipality in the later stages of the development process. The growing importance of pre-application discussions, as a result of the Planning Delivery Grants, and the intention to keep the planning policies (Local Development Frameworks) more up-to-date than the development plans used to be, should result in 'front-loading', which means that transaction costs of development control itself should be reduced and shifted to an earlier stage in the process.

The Netherlands and Houston have a system that is based primarily on legal certainty, with an emphasis on codified planning regulations. If an application fits within the planning and building requirements, permission has to be granted, and if it does not, permission has to be refused. For the Netherlands, this is at least the situation on paper. In practice, the certainty that is provided is not as great as one would expect. There are many possibilities for deviating from the plan, and many plans (because of their generally high level of detail) are not made in advance, but are put in place or changed when a developer or the municipality comes up with a development initiative. This has led in the city of Nijmegen to the existence of 600 *bestemmingsplannen*, most of which are older than the required 10 years (under the existing act, the plans do not lose their validity if they are not renewed). Therefore, the presumed association with the 'rule of law' is characterised instead as 'the big lie' (Needham, 2006a). Although the system is not as rigid, or trustworthy, or predictable, as it might seem, the way that changes are made to the user rights regime are along the lines of the formal-legal procedures. This means that local authorities can deviate from the existing regime, but only after the changes have gone through a prescribed procedure, with room for third party involvement. This makes it probably more transaction-cost consuming than the English system, but also less arbitrary.

Closely related to the previous point, is the difference in the language and the style in which regulations are written the Netherlands and the US on the one hand, and England on the other. This is the result of the role of the plan in the system. The plan in England is a policy document, while in the US and the Netherlands it has the legal status of planning law. In the English case, the planning regulations are sometimes written in broad multi-interpretable terms, especially in the local plans and local development frameworks, but also in the planning conditions and section 106 agreements. In the Netherlands and the US, *bestemmingsplannen*, zoning and development ordinances and building permissions are written by lawyers, while in England they are produced by policy-makers that often have a planning background: this leads to flexible planning guidance, but also to ambiguous messages from local authorities to developers. This can be particularly problematic when planning permissions are granted. Many planning conditions and obligations that are attached to the planning permission are subject to interpretation and discussion, after permission has been granted. Research by Adair *et al.* (1998), on private investments in land and property, demonstrates the importance of clarity in public policies in reducing risk and uncertainties for developers and investors.

Of the three case studies, the city of Houston provides the most certainty for developers. The regulations are relatively stable, generic (that is, city-wide) and not location-specific, and written down in an unambiguous way. The transaction costs borne by the developers that are related to the user rights regime are therefore relatively low. At the same time, the regime is very permissive, since many developments, or land uses, are allowed. The flip side is that the city of Houston is not accountable to third parties, like neighbouring landowners and other stakeholders, for incompatible land uses (apart from some exceptions). One of the main aims of planning in many developed countries is internalising externalities, and related to that, being accountable if two land uses that do not fit are located next to each other. To a large extent, the privately set up restrictive covenants cover this problem, since these regulate the externality issue at the level of the location to which covenant is concerned. But problems sometimes arise when conflicts emerge between areas, as demonstrated in the previous section by the example of the development project that was withdrawn in Rice Village, as a result of an insurmountable conflict with the neighbourhood. This leads indirectly to more transaction costs that should also be taken into the equation.

# References

Adair, A., Berry, J., Deddis, S., McGreal, S. & Hirst, S. (1998) *Assessing Private Finance: The Availability and Effectiveness of Private Finance in Urban Regeneration*. RICS, London.

Adams, D., Disberry, A., Hutchison, N. & Munjoma, T. (2001) Managing urban land: the case for urban partnership zones. *Regional Studies* **35**(2): 153–62.

Adams, D., Disberry, A., Hutchison, N. & Munjoma, T. (2002) Land policy and urban renaissance: the impact of ownership constraints in four British cities. *Planning Theory and Practice* **3**(2): 195–217.

Allmendinger, P. & Ball, M. (2006) *New Horizons Research Programme. Rethinking the Planning Regulation of Land and Property Markets*. Office of the Deputy Prime Minister, London.

Arup (2004) *Investigating The Increasing Volume of Planning Appeals*. Office of the Deputy Prime Minister, London.

Askew, J. & Hartogs, C. (2005) *The Involvement of Consultants in the Dutch Planning System: Briefing Paper for the Audit Commission*. Audit Commision, Wetherby.

Audit Commission (2006a) *Corporate Assessment Bristol City Council*. Audit Commission, London.

Audit Commission (2006b) *The Planning System: Matching Expectations and Capacity*. Audit Commission Publications, Wetherby.

Ben-Joseph, E. (2003) *Subdivision Regulations: Practices and Attitudes*. Lincoln Institute of Land Policy, Working Paper, Boston MA.

Burning, B. & Glasson, J. (2004) *Skill Base in the Planning System: A Literature Review*. Local Government Association, London.

CBI (2005) CBI Response to: *Further Proposed Changes to the System of Planning Fees in England* – Consultation paper. CBI, London.

Cullingworth, B. & Nadin, V. (2006) *Town & Country Planning in the UK*, 14th edn. Routledge, London.

De Bruijn, J. A., De Jong, P., Korsten, A. F. A. & Van Zanten, W. P. C. (eds) (1996) *Grote Projecten: Besluitvorming & Management*. Samsom H.D. Tjeenk Willink, Alphen aan den Rijn.

Faludi, A. (2005) The Netherlands: a culture with a soft spot for planning. In: B. Sanyal (ed.), *Comparative Planning Cultures*, Routledge, New York, pp. 285–307.

Faludi, A. & Van der Valk, A. (1994) *Rule and Order; Dutch Planning Doctrine in the Twentieth Century*. Kluwer Academic, Dordrech.

Feagin, J. R. (1988) *Free Enterprise City: Houston in Political and Economic Perspective*. Rutgers University, New Brunswick, NJ/London.

Hajer, M., Sijmons, D. & Feddes, F. (eds) (2006) *Een Plan dat Werkt: Ontwerp en Politiek in Regionale Planvorming*. NAi Uitgevers, Rotterdam.

HMSO (1985) Lifting the Burden, *White Paper*. HMSO, London.

Houston Chronicle (2005) Developer calls off high-rise project; residential units near Rice Village no longer planned, 16 January.

McKenzie, E. (2003) Common-interest housing in the communities of tomorrow, *Housing Policy Debate* **14**(1 and 2): 203–34.

Nadin, V., Hawkes, P., Cooper, S., Shaw, D. & Westlake, T. (1997) *The EU Compendium of Spatial Planning Systems, Regional Development Studies 28*. European Commission, Brussels.

Needham, B. (2006a) The new Dutch spatial planning act: continuity and change in the way in which the Dutch regulate the practice of spatial planning. *Planning Practice and Research* **20**(3): 327–40.

Needham, B. (2006b) *Planning, Law and Economics: The Rules We Make for Using Land*. Routledge, London.

Neuman, M. (2003b) *Planning the City without a Plan*, paper presented at the AESOP-ACSP Congress. Leuven, 8–12 July.

Nijland, H. G. M. (2005) Ontwikkelingen rond de apparaatskosten bij de bouwgrondproductie. *Achtergrondinformatie* (2): 43–52.

ODPM (2004) A*n Overview of Planning Standards Authorities 2003/04*. Office of the Deputy Prime Minister, London.

ODPM (2005a) *Evaluation of Planning Delivery Grant 2004/05*. Office of the Deputy Prime Minister, London.

ODPM (2005b) *Information on Calculating Provisional Development Control, Enterprise Areas and Appeal Abatements Elements of PDG 2006/07*. Office of the Deputy Prime Minister, London.

ODPM (2005c) *An Overview of Planning Standards Authorities 2004/05*. Office of the Deputy Prime Minister, London.

Planning Inspectorate (2005) *Annual Reports and Accounts 2004/05*. The Stationery Office, London.

Sanyal, B. (eds) (2005) *Comparative Planning Cultures*. Routledge, New York.

Scharpf, F. (1997) *Games Real Actors Play: Actor-Centered Institutionalism in Policy Research*. Westview Press, Boulder CO.

Seidel, S. (1978) *Housing Costs and Government Regulations: Confronting the Regulatory Maze*. Centre for Urban Policy Research, Rutgers University, New Brunswick NJ.

The Mayor's Building Permit Task Force (2004) *Promoting Responsible Development within the City of Houston: Reforming the City's Building Permit Process*. City of Houston, Houston TX.

Van Ark, R. (2005) *Planning, Contract en Commitment: Naar een Relationeel Perspectief op Gebiedscontracten in de Ruimtelijke Planning.* Eburon, Delft.

Van Hoek, B. (2004) Plankosten voor ruimtelijke ontwikkelingen. *SerVicE*, **12**(1): 29–31.

VROM-raad (2004) *Gereedschap voor Ruimtelijke Ontwikkelingspolitiek.* VROM-raad, Den Haag.

# 9

# Planning at What Cost? Conclusions and Discussion

Transaction cost theory offers a very interesting vocabulary for investigating property development practices. In this study, I have applied transaction cost economics – which is usually applied in business studies, organisation studies and applied economics – to land use planning and land development. This branch of planning and property research is relatively new, and there are very few empirical studies. I have suggested some modifications to transaction cost economics, based on insights from the original institutional economics, economic sociology and sociological institutionalism. The two most important modifications concern the assumptions about human behaviour and the multiplicity of institutions. Transaction cost economics assumes that agents act autonomously, based on an economic rationality, with only one goal: utility maximisation. But economists like Veblen drew our attention to irrational behaviour, such as, what he called, 'conspicuous behaviour'. More importantly, we have learned that behaviour is not autonomous and unconstrained but is embedded and institutionalised. Institutions reveal themselves at many levels and in many different forms, with complicated relationships between them. Due to this institutional complexity, we cannot explain transaction costs in a particular development process just by referring to the costs produced by the governance structures chosen for that process. So this book has posed the following questions: how are the different institutional levels and transaction costs interrelated under different circumstances, and how does this affect the existence, size and incidence of transaction costs in the development process?

In Chapter 3, I operationalised governance structures in what I called 'user rights regimes', which could be seen as the formal rules that restrict and define the way land can be used and exchanged in a particular location. This user rights regime is mainly created and used during the development process, but within the public and private law rules are set at the meso level. The pilot case, literature review and the first experiences with the case studies pointed out that, in general, we can distinguish four stages in the development process in which the user rights regime is used and created. These stages are land exchange, making or changing a land use plan, drawing up an agreement about how the land should be used, and finally the planning or building permission stage. These four stages can be used to analyse development practices. It must be noted that these four are not always present. In the Houston case, for instance, there was no land use plan and none was made. Neither was there an agreement similar to the section 106 agreement in the Bristol case or the development agreement in the Nijmegen case. Some of these differences can be explained by the differences in institutions at the meso level.

User rights regimes are created within the limits of the formal rules of the game. These limits allow choices to be made for a particular development process (that is, the micro level). Transaction costs are the result of the actions by agents within the development process. There is much specificity in the cases that has an influence on transaction costs. An example is the attitude of the developer at Wapping Wharf that led to much opposition from the residents, which led to a delay. Interfin decided to design its condominiums after the example of another project – Villa d'Este – that was constructed some years earlier. And in the Dutch case, there were some problems with the land acquisition that caused delays.

These actions by the agents involved in the development process are, however, influenced by factors that go beyond the site and the individual level. In Chapter 7, I identified four key dimensions from, what I have called, the macro level, that affect the existence, size and incidence of transaction costs; namely the quest for control, the relationship between public and private, the attitudes towards transaction costs, and the legal style. The four dimensions, which have been elaborated in Chapter 8, are major discriminating factors between the way development is carried out in the three cities and the three countries. The insights that are derived from this study offer interesting perspectives on transaction cost economics, theoretically, methodologically and ontologically. Although the vocabulary of transaction cost theory offers useful analytical tools, I deviate from the basic causal relations that the theory makes between the central concepts.

## Applying transaction cost theory to planning and development

### Institutions and transaction costs

In Chapter 2, the relationship between institutions and transaction costs was discussed. One observation is that institutions do not only reduce transaction costs, but increase them also. Governance structures are not only used to facilitate exchange, and economise on transaction costs, they are also used to exercise power and restrict others, irrespective of the transaction costs that they produce.

Starting with *The nature of the firm* by Coase (1937), organisations (like firms) and institutions are treated as devices that facilitate exchange, by reducing transaction costs. If the costs of exchanging through the market becomes too high, the firm becomes an appropriate governance structure. However, reducing transaction costs is not the only reason for the existence of and changes to institutions. Zoning, planning conditions, planning obligations, expropriation and so forth, which are all public law tools, are not only (or maybe not often) devised to facilitate exchange, they are primarily used to influence the behaviour of others in a direction that is desired by the planning agency that sets them up, often irrespective of the transaction costs they cause.

Related to that, transaction costs are generally seen as costs that are made in reaction to external factors (like interdependencies, uncertainty and timing) and the internal human features (like opportunism and bounded rationality). Actors respond and adapt to these circumstances – that is, both the external factors and the human features – and that lead to transaction costs. Following from this, differences in transaction costs can be explained by differences in these factors. But this says very little about why and to what end human actors want to design governance structures. The wish of an (public) agency to have *control* over the outcome of a development process, and hence over the actions of others, seems to be the most important driving force behind transaction costs.

I conclude tentatively from this study that it is the level of control that local authorities particularly want to exercise which is the main discriminating factor for the difference in transaction costs (there does not seem to be a lot of difference – in the case studies – in the way that developers want to control the outcome). Gaining control is what a transaction is about. The level is of control is not static and changes over time. In addition, it is relational and dependent on the relative power of other agencies. This power-oriented perspective is close to Pearce's view (Pearce, 2005), who criticises transaction cost economics for its premise that institutions move towards reducing transaction costs and increasing efficiency. Rather, institutions like the example he uses of the English planning system, change as a result of a change in the balance of power in society.

If institutions, organisations and even cities, as it is sometimes argued (see e.g. Webster & Lai, 2003), always move towards economising on and reducing transaction costs, then why is there any diversity between cities, institutions and organisations? The problem with transaction cost economics and mainstream economics is that it is a-historical (Hodgson, 2004). Each city and each nation develops its own culture. As we have seen in Chapter 8, the three cities can be differently characterised.

But even if the claim of many transaction cost economists is right, namely that institutions change so as to reduce transaction costs, it still does not tell us much about how, when and under which circumstances institutions change, nor who changes them. Transaction costs are part of a wider range of factors, and are not one single determining factor.

### Remediableness: a difficult criterion

Williamson's remediableness criterion, which has been adopted by Alexander (2001a)[1], is applied to the choice between alternative feasible, real-life, institutional arrangements, by comparing the transaction costs they produce, and holding the output and all other circumstances constant. The arrangement that produces the given output with the least transaction costs is assumed to be most efficient.

However, what the cases have shown is that although the output at the project level might be similar (that is, housing projects of around

---

[1] In some previous publications (Buitelaar, 2003, 2004), I also endorsed it as a promising concept.

100 units)², the output at the city level might be quite different. There is not much difference in the quality of the three projects, however that is measured; this could lead to the conclusion that the user rights regime of Montebello in Houston is most efficient, because it had the lowest transaction costs. The absence of zoning saves costs in the individual housing project, since the building application does not need to be subjected to a zoning review. However, the absence of zoning reveals itself not only at the site level. There are also transaction costs that are dispersed among the landowners within one neighbourhood who enter into restrictive covenants with their neighbours to prevent or reduce negative externalities. Other costs are those that both neighbourhoods and developers bear when they argue over or negotiate land uses that are locally unwanted. Zoning would make the city of Houston accountable for the land use designations and could save costs for the landowners.

A user rights regime is inevitably connected to higher-level institutions (like zoning laws) that have their influence not only on the user rights regime in one location, but on all the user rights regimes in a city, village or the whole country. This means that the outcome of a local user rights regime has to be assessed not just at the local level. When we move up the spatial scale, towards the city or national level, we see quite different results in each of the three cities and countries. The lack of zoning, but more importantly the weakly developed planning culture and the strongly developed growth culture in Houston, give the city a pro-growth image, in which the City of Houston refrains from controlling in detail the actions of landowners, and hence the spatial output. The Netherlands is seen as a country that endorses values such as integration and order (Faludi & Van Der Valk, 1994) in its spatial structure, two things that are less apparent in Houston and Bristol. One could argue that this seemingly costly integrated-comprehensive approach (Nadin *et al.*, 1997) produces a higher quality, and hence a different output. But it must be said that this is difficult to prove, since not only beauty, but also quality, is in the eye of the beholder.

---

² It must be said that although the cases have a similar housing program, small locational differences can have significant consequences for the transactions, such as soil that is contaminated or a site that lies (partly) on a flood plain.

Neither the spatial output nor the institutional arrangements stand on their own, but are related to other outputs and arrangements (i.e the institutional environment) at other levels. This makes an evaluation of remediableness at one level, without taking account of other levels, inadequate, at least, as a methodology for land use planning and land development.

Another issue of which remediableness, and transaction cost theory in general, takes very little notice is the incidence of the transaction costs. Who bears the costs and who has power over whom to determine that incidence? What might be efficient for one party might be highly inefficient for the other (Keogh & D'arcy, 1999). If we look at the Dutch case, we see that although the municipality bore a lot of transaction costs during the process, it has been able to recoup a large share from the developer in the form of fees and contributions in the development agreement. This was possible because the developer was able to rely on the cooperation of the city. This means that the municipality does not need to be bothered by high transaction costs, because it can rely on its power position to recover those costs. In the Netherlands, this seems to be especially the case with smaller projects that do not have high political priority and in which the municipality does not bear any risks. If the municipality is not actively involved in acquiring and developing the land, it does not have the risk of incurring interest costs that are caused by delays. Without these costs and with the certainty, when municipal cooperation is required to change the user rights regime, and to recoup the costs it makes during the process, local authorities do not seem to be concerned about duration and transaction costs. Transaction cost theory assumes an equal drive among stakeholders to economise on transaction costs. This takes too little notice of differences in interest and power.

## The ontology of transaction cost economics

Governance structures, and institutions in general, do not cause transaction costs. It is the way in which institutions are created and used that determines the transaction costs. This dynamic and constructivist view on institutions is important to avoid the pitfall of a deterministic view on institutions. Institutions are social constructions, and so are transaction costs.

This does not, however, mean that the actor can optimise his choices at will. What became clear in the case studies (and Buitelaar *et al.*, 2006), in relation to transaction cost theory, is the importance of acknowledging Giddens' duality of structure. Transaction cost theory implicitly assumes that governance structures are 'chosen' voluntarily. But this choice is never unconstrained. This view ignores the role of structures and it is therefore an undersocialised view of human behaviour. We need to take account of what Hodgson calls 'cumulative downward causation' (see Chapter 2), which comes down to the notion that individuals are not rational actors that live only in the moment, but are historically and institutionally embedded. Dependencies, relations, conventions, rules and so on have an important influence on the way actors behave. Therefore user rights regimes, and institutional arrangements in general, are not chosen freely from an unlimited number of alternatives, but are created out of a limited range of alternatives. This limits the capacity to influence transaction costs as they are embedded in an institutional and relational context. In line with Furubotn (1997), I argue that new institutional economists should try to disassociate themselves more from neo-classical economics and its assumptions on rationality. It is important not to overemphasise the role of institutions (which is done by methodological collectivists), because human behaviour and its results are not dictated by structures. But structures do make certain actions and outcomes – like the size and the incidence of transaction costs – more likely than others.

In the field of planning and property, more research should be done on how people are related, how they interact and how institutions shape that interaction. This should be done on an even more detailed level than is done in this study. Ethnographic research in particular could help to unravel the informal links and rules of the game between people. This could complement mainstream economic analyses.

## Transaction costs as dead weight losses or means with a purpose?

Transaction cost economics, when applied normatively, tends to emphasise that transaction costs ought to be reduced, in order to allow exchange to proceed more smoothly, which should ultimately lead to a higher level of allocative efficiency. The assumption behind this seems to be that transaction costs are dead weight losses. But what about the benefits associated with them? Sometimes the costs can be high; but the benefits of incurring these costs can be high as well (see also, Pearce, 2005). Below, I discuss two topical issues where there is a clear trade-off between the costs and the benefits.

### Spatial quality/order: control over space has a price

There are differences in the spatial structure between Nijmegen, Bristol and Houston, partly because of a difference in planning style. The Dutch 'integrated-comprehensive' approach differs from the English 'land use management' (see, for both labels Nadin *et al.*, 1997), and the Houstonian 'privately led development' approach.

The transaction costs associated with the way the Dutch carry out spatial planning appear to be high. This is closely related to the ambitions they have for space and related to that, the quest for control over space. The wish for rule and order seems to justify sometimes immense planning departments (see Appendix B). Transaction costs are subordinate to concepts like spatial order. Currently, both the ambitions and the size of bureaucracy are under pressure. The ambitions and goals are being moderated due to a political neo-liberal discourse and the increased importance of private parties on the land market. Bureaucracy is under pressure because of the economic depression in the early years of the new millennium and the reduction in tax incomes as a result. In addition, it has been one of the key issues on the agenda of the Balkenende cabinet that came to power in 2002.

The ambitions in English planning after World War II have been lower than in Dutch planning, especially during the Thatcher era. Planning has long been confined to land use management or, in other words, a way of planning that tries to do no more than preventing incompatible land uses from developing next to each other. However, there is an emerging discourse in which concepts such as forward planning, sustainability, integration, spatial planning (instead of land use) are gaining ground. To live up to the expectations that have been raised by the adoption of the 2004 Planning and Compulsory Purchase Act, the capacity, and hence the transaction costs, have to be raised. Central government deliberately wants to raise transaction costs, although it obviously prefers to use the word capacity, to achieve the ambitions it has put forward.

The costs related to public planning appear to be lower in Houston than in the Dutch and English situation, and this perhaps counts for most American cities. The kind of public controls that most European countries have are absent in most US cities (see also Pearce, 2005).

But at the same time, there are many people who are sceptical about the quality of the American cities and villages, which are contemptuously called 'anywhere' or 'nowhere' America. Kunstler (2001) cynically and provocatively compares American cities with Berlin, that has recovered from World War II and is recovering from the post-war division, by saying that:

> `[...] Cleveland, St. Louis, Baltimore, Detroit, Buffalo, Hartford, Indianapolis, Nashville, *Houston*, Birmingham, Richmond, Raleigh, Topeka, Des Moines, Scranton, Worcester, Louisville, and other cities of the victorious United States, leader of the Free World, look as if the enemy bombers flew over them yesterday.'
>
> (Kunstler, 2001, p. 140)

Owing to suburbanisation and edge city developments, cities, city centres and city life have come under pressure, something which is clearly visible in Houston as well[3]. Urban problems seem to be much more profound and severe than in Western Europe. In the past, the city of Houston hardly stimulated spatial and economic development in the core of the city, and actively facilitated suburban development including the Galleria area (the area surrounding Montebello), Houston's famous edge city (Garreau, 1988). The city centre has become an area where hardly anybody lives, with very few cultural, retail and other facilities, and which is dominated by offices and parking lots. This makes it a surreal and spooky place to be at night. The situation is probably even worse in the fringe that surrounds downtown (just outside the Interstate Highway 610), where many sites are vacant, derelict and neglected[4]. Economising on (transaction) costs in planning can mean high (social) costs in the end, as Donald Shoup also emphasised in his book *The High Cost Of Free Parking* (Shoup, 2005). In this book, he demonstrates what supplying ample freely accessible parking space in the US means in terms of congestion, energy use and urban development. This leads to the question of what the costs are, in terms of

---

[3] This is something that American scholars and practitioners try to come to terms with in developments such as growth management, smart growth and new urbanism.

[4] Robert Campbell says about the perception of cites: 'The city has become, in the American imagination, the place where foreigners live. It is the place where people have funny accents, worship strange gods, and probably can't be entirely trusted.' (quoted in Kunstler, 2001, p. 195)

spatial and environmental quality, of the wish to leave as much as possible to the discretion of commercial developers. However, this question has very little priority in Houston, where many celebrate the motto 'industry was a man's occupation, and it was never meant to be pretty'. (Neuman, 2003b) High ambitions go along with high transaction costs. But it was Sir Henry Royce, co-founder of Rolls-Royce, who said: 'The quality remains long after the price has been forgotten'.

### Legitimacy: collaborative planning at what cost?

Public participation, for instance in the form of a local public inquiry or in more informal sessions led by a mediator (as at Wapping Wharf), can have various benefits (Henneberry, 2005). People can exercise their civic rights, plans can be improved (due to involving more creative minds), decisions are better informed and plans more likely receive acceptance and support from the local community. However, there is also a downside related to this.

One of the dominant paradigms within planning theory at the moment is the communicative or collaborative paradigm (Healey, 1997; Innes & Booher, 2003), in which interactive processes are advocated. The planning process has no pre-established goal, and the outcome of the process is the result of the interaction between the actors involved. This might be a major step forward compared to the monocentric and technocratic process view that dominated the 1960s and the 1970s. However, deliberation, consultation and negotiation are not without costs. The more people who are involved, the more opinions and interests there are, and the more likely it becomes that conflicts of interest arise that give rise to transaction costs. Community involvement and stakeholder participation in general is often discussed as benevolent for both process and outcome, but it can have disadvantages for the duration and the process costs.

On the other hand, planning agencies might incur transaction costs not only to achieve quality and legitimacy, but also to preserve their own bureaucracies. Bureaucracy has gained a negative connotation, but Max Weber showed that it could be seen as a rational from of organisation, compared to 'the market' (Parsons, 1995). This line could be extended to transaction cost theory, by which the government can be seen as a specific type of firm that exists to reduce transaction costs of private persons and firms. Public choice theorists (see e.g. Downs, 1967) are, however, more sceptical about the purposes of public bureaucracies; they question whether government agencies serve the public interest. In their view, public bureaucracies serve their own interest, which reveals itself in ever-expanding bureaucratic organisations, also at the local level, notwithstanding the cutbacks or other restrictions that are imposed by for instance the national government. As we saw the Chapter 8, some cities do not choose to make the transaction cost streams more transparent, because that would most likely reveal inefficiencies, and related to that, redundancies.

In the case studies there were examples of transaction costs that could be attributed to inefficiencies. In the Bristol case, we see a lot of correspondence and discussion on planning conditions and conformance to these conditions, before they can be discharged. In the Dutch case, it takes at least four years before some tangible commitment between the city of Nijmegen and the developer is created. And in the Houston case, the developer decided to slow down the process to wait for momentum in the real estate market (more specifically the market for condominiums) to sell the units[5].

The question is: how to draw the boundary between functional costs and dead-weight costs? And who is to judge? It is beneficial in many cases to make an explicit trade-off between what you want to achieve and what that would cost in transactions. I am not making a plea for calculated behaviour of planners in every decision, because that would make them accountants and kill creativity and out-of-the-box thinking. But it is sometimes good to appreciate that everything has its price. This does not always imply that the institutional arrangement with the least transaction costs should be chosen. Sometimes it is appropriate to incur transaction costs in planning for the longer term benefits that it can bring to society through a better way of using land.

# References

Alexander, E. R. (2001a) A transaction-cost theory of land use planning and development control. Toward the institutional analysis of public planning. *Town Planning Review* **72**(1): 45–75.

Buitelaar, E. (2003) Neither market nor government. Comparing the performance of user rights regimes. *Town Planning Review* **74**(3): 315–30.

---

[5] However, this cannot be attributed to the user rights regime.

Buitelaar, E. (2004) A transaction-cost analysis of the land development process. *Urban Studies* **41**(13): 2539–53.

Buitelaar, E., Mertens, H., Needham, B. & De Kam, G. (2006) *Sturend Vermogen en Woningbouw: Een Onderzoek Naar het Vermogen van Gemeenten Om te Sturen bij de Ontwikkeling van Woningbouwlocaties.* DGW/NETHUR, Den Haag/Utrecht.

Coase, R. H. (1937) The nature of the firm. *Economica* **4**(16): 386–405.

Downs, A. (1967) *Inside Bureaucracy.* Little, Boston MA.

Faludi, A. & Van der Valk, A. (1994) *Rule and Order; Dutch Planning Doctrine in the Twentieth Century.* Kluwer Academic Publishers, Dordrecht.

Furubotn, E. G. (1997) The old and the new institutionalism in economics. In: P. Koslowski (ed.) *Methodology of the Social Sciences, Ethics, and Economics in the Newer Historical School: From Max Weber and Rickert to Sombart and Rothacker,* Springer, Berlin, pp. 429–63.

Garreau, J. (1988) *Edge City: Life on the New Frontier.* Doubleday, New York.

Healey, P. (1997) *Collaborative Planning: Shaping Places in Fragmented Societies.* Macmillan, Basingstoke.

Henneberry, J. (2005) Engaging planning with economics. *Town Planning Review* **76**(4): 493–4.

Hodgson, G. M. (2004) *The Evolution of Institutional Economics: Agency, Structure and Darwinism in American Institutionalism.* Routledge, London.

Innes, J. E. & Booher, D. E. (2003) Collaborative policymaking: governance through dialogue, In: M. Hajer & H. Wagenaar (eds), *Deliberative Policy Analysis, Understanding Governance in the Network Society,* Cambridge University Press, Cambridge.

Keogh, G. & d'Arcy, É. (1999) Property market efficiency: an institutional economics perspective. *Urban Studies* **36**(13): 2401–14.

Kunstler, J. H. (2001) *The City in Mind: Notes on the Urban Condition.* The Free Press, New York.

Nadin, V., Hawkes, P., Cooper, S., Shaw, D. & Westlake, T. (1997) *The EU Compendium of Spatial Planning Systems, Regional Development Studies 28.* European Commission, Brussels.

Neuman, M. (2003b) *Planning the City without a Plan* Paper presented at the AESOP-ACSP Congress. Leuven, 8–12 July.

Parsons, W. (1995) *Public Policy. An Introduction to the Theory and Practice of Policy Analysis.* Edward Elgar, Cheltenham/Northampton MA.

Pearce, B. (2005) Balancing efficiency in planning with justice, power and culture. *Town Planning Review* **76**(4): 488–92.

Shoup, D. C. (2005) *The High Cost of Free Parking.* APA, Chicago IL.

Webster, C. J. & Lai, L. W. C. (2003) *Property Rights, Planning and Markets: Managing Spontaneous Cities.* Edward Elgar, Cheltenham/Northampton MA.

# Appendix A: Interviewees

| Interviewee | Affiliation | Date interview |
|---|---|---|
| *The Netherlands* | | |
| Cees Zoon | Municipality of Nijmegen | 08-09-2003 |
| Peter Jensen | Municipality of Nijmegen | 28-03-2006 |
| Wout van Hees | Municipality of Nijmegen | 15-09-2003/09-01-2004 |
| Jan Alberts | Municipality of Nijmegen | 30-03-2006 |
| Ramon Kemperman | Municipality of Nijmegen | 30-03-2006 |
| Rene Schippers | KDO developers | 16-01-2004 |
| Bram de Deugd | Municipality of Hilversum | 05-08-2003 |
| Henk-Jan Oostlander | Municipality of Hilversum | 12-08-2003 |
| Rene van der Straaten | Metafoor consultants / Municipality of Doetinchem | 12-10-2005 |
| Chantal Robbe | Municipality of Den Haag | 05-04-2006 |
| Ad van der Ven | Akro Consult | 04-04-2006 |
| Hans Voesenek | Municipality of Breda | 06-04-2006 |
| Gerrit Verkerk | Ecorys | 03-04-2006 |
| Jan Fokkema | NEPROM | 19-04-2006 |
| *England* | | |
| Nigel Honer | Bruges Tozer architects | 19-05-2004 |
| Wayne Window | Bristol City Council | 17-05-2004 |
| Bryan Cadman | Bristol City Council | 03-07-2006 |
| Mass Palacco | Beaufort Homes | 06-05-2004 |
| Ian Thomas | Beaufort Homes | 08-05-2004 |
| Janet Askew | University of the West of England | various times |
| Mike Devereux | University of the West of England | various times |
| Vincent Nadin | University of the West of England | various times |
| Christine Lambert | University of the West of England | various times |
| Neil Harris | Cardiff University | 17-05-2006 |
| Wayne Dyer | ARUP | 18-05-2006 |
| Eamon Mythen | ODPM | 19-05-2006 |
| *Houston* | | |
| Cecilia Giusti | Texas A&M University | various times |
| Dawn Jourdan | Texas A&M University | various times |
| Atef Sharkawi | Texas A&M University | various times |
| Micheal Neuman | Texas A&M University | various times |
| Georgio Borlenghi | Interfin | 05-04-2005 |
| Kyle Styles | Interfin | 04-05-2005/21-05-2005 |
| Dan Pruitt | City of Houston | 26-04-2005 |
| Sheila Blake | City of Houston | 26-04-2005 |
| Suzy Hartgrove | City of Houston | 31-03-2005/15-04-2005 |
| Amar Mohite | City of Houston | 31-03-2005 |

# Appendix B:   People Working in Planning

It is difficult to identify, and practically nearly impossible to quantify, the transaction costs of a user rights regime let alone a whole planning system. A good indicator, however, of the transaction costs that are related to land use planning is the size of the planning department. As we see in, for instance, Chapter 8, a good transaction cost analysis almost requires a whole government evaluation. This is obviously impossible, but a comparison of the size of local planning departments in the three countries might shed a light on the costs associated with the way planning is carried out.

The problem is that often there is no such thing as a 'planning department', and if there is, it might not include the exact same activities as in other planning departments, not even in the same country, let alone in other countries. Therefore I have chosen to investigate how many people are working on various planning and related tasks. The categories that have been chosen are:

- strategic planning (including transport, housing, heritage, public space, environmental and economic policy)
- making the land use regulations (zoning, *bestemmingsplan*, etc.)
- project development (active land development by the city)
- plan review (zoning, platting, building regulations, environmental regulations, etc.)
- inspections (on building and environmental regulations)

These categories do not include the design, construction and maintenance of real estate, public space and infrastructure by local authorities, but are in essence only the 'soft' side of development.

Although the investigation has been done thoroughly, it is impossible to prevent omissions and overlap entirely. For instance, if in one municipality all the categories are clustered in one planning department, the overhead is also counted, but when all four categories are part of four bigger separate departments the overhead is not taken into account because it then also concerns the other activities in the department. Because of this, the data should be seen as *indications* of the size of the planning departments.

The information was collected by detailed analysis of organisation structures on websites, and by over 100 phone calls and numerous e-mails. The cities investigated should not be seen as representative for their country. Cities from the top 10 – population-wise – in each country have been chosen, including Houston, Nijmegen and Bristol. It proved to be difficult to acquire the information for all the top 10 cities. Therefore, only the cities that were able to provide accurate information are shown.

## Netherlands[1]

Collecting the data for the Dutch planning departments proved to be the most difficult of all countries. Rotterdam and Amsterdam, in particular, have a nearly impenetrable municipal organisation: they have decentralised many activities. In absolute terms, this means extra bureaucracy/overhead. In Amsterdam, the municipal land department alone employs 433 people, against 434 in Rotterdam.

## England[2]

In England, the numbers – related to the population N are much lower than in the Netherlands (see also Table B.4). One reason could be the

**Table B.1**  Planning departments in the Netherlands

| Cities | City population 2005[a] | 'Planning department'[b] | Inhabitants per planning official |
|---|---|---|---|
| 1. Amsterdam | 742,783 | 1910 | 389 |
| 2. Rotterdam | 596,407 | 1413 | 422 |
| 3. Den Haag | 472,096 | 915 | 516 |
| 4. Utrecht | 275,258 | 780 | 353 |
| 5. Eindhoven | 208,455 | 280 | 744 |
| 9. Breda | 168,054 | 230 | 731 |
| 10. Nijmegen | 158,215 | 400 | 396 |

[a] http://www.cbs.nl
[b] The data for this were collected in January 2006

---

[1] I am grateful to Harm Mertens for his help with finding the data for the Dutch cities.
[2] I am grateful to Bas Zonnenberg for his help with finding the data for the English cities.

**Table B.2**   Planning departments in England

| Cities[a] | City population 2001[b] | 'Planning department'[c] | Inhabitants per planning official |
|---|---|---|---|
| 2. Birmingham | 970,892 | 254 | 3822 |
| 4. Leeds | 443,247 | 254 | 1745 |
| 5. Sheffield | 439,866 | 230 | 1912 |
| 6. Bristol | 420,556 | 228 | 1845 |

[a] They are all unitary authorities.
[b] http://www.statistics.gov.uk
[c] The data for this were collected in June and July 2006

general lack of planners, which makes most planning departments short-staffed. Another major difference is the number of people working in forward – or strategic – planning. To give one example, the city of Leeds, a city with over 400,000 inhabitants, has 73 people working in forward planning, while the city of Nijmegen, which has 40% of the the population of Leeds, employs over 150 people in this area.

## USA

US planning departments seem to be smallest, when related to the population (see also Table B.4). Even more than in the English cities, this is because of the limited number of people working in strategic planning and in active project development and management. Of the 380 people working in planning in Houston, only 80 of them deal with policy making, neighbourhood initiatives, historic preservations, economic planning and so on.

Neuman (2003a) wrote that Houston has the biggest planning department of the US. But this is a matter of how you measure.

**Table B.3**   Planning departments in the US

| Cities | City population 2003[a] | 'Planning department'[b] | Inhabitants per planning official |
|---|---|---|---|
| 1. New York | 8,085,742 | 1220 | 6628 |
| 2. Los Angeles | 3,819,951 | 1160 | 3293 |
| 4. Houston | 2,009,690 | 380 | 5289 |
| 8. San Antonio | 1,214,725 | 260 | 4672 |
| 9. Dallas | 1,208,318 | 330 | 3662 |

[a] http://www.citypopulation.de/USA.html
[b] The data for this were collected in May 2005.

**Table B.4**   Planning departments compared, from 'small' to 'big', related to the population

| Cities | City population 2003[a] | 'Planning department'[b] | Inhabitants per planning officer |
|---|---|---|---|
| New York | 8,085,742 | 1220 | 6628 |
| Houston | 2,009,690 | 380 | 5289 |
| San Antonio | 1,214,725 | 260 | 4672 |
| Birmingham | 970,892 | 254 | 3822 |
| Dallas | 1,208,318 | 330 | 3662 |
| Los Angeles | 3,819,951 | 1160 | 3293 |
| Sheffield | 439,866 | 230 | 1912 |
| Bristol | 420,556 | 228 | 1845 |
| Leeds | 443,247 | 254 | 1745 |
| Eindhoven | 208.455 | 280 | 744 |
| Breda | 168.054 | 230 | 731 |
| Den Haag | 472.096 | 915 | 516 |
| Rotterdam | 596.407 | 1413 | 422 |
| Nijmegen | 158.215 | 400 | 396 |
| Amsterdam | 742.783 | 1910 | 389 |
| Utrecht | 275.258 | 780 | 353 |

[a] http://www.citypopulation.de/USA.html
[b] The data for this were collected in May 2005

Before October 2004, the Department of Planning and Development of the City of Houston had around 380 employees. By comparison, the Department of City Planning of New York City employed 334 people in 2005. But 300 of the 380 people in Houston's planning department worked in the division of code enforcement: they dealt with plan reviews, inspections, and the issuance of building permits and certificates of occupancy. In October 2004 this division was taken out of the planning department and joined with the Department of Public Works and Engineering, leaving the planning department with only 80 people. If one looks at the kind of activities that the code enforcement division does, and searches for the department that does that in New York City, the Department of Buildings will be found, which has a total number of 885 people who do the inspections and the plan reviews, adding up to a total of 1220 people doing similar activities as the 380 in Houston. In the case of New York there are various housing departments, like New York City Housing Authority (NYCHA) and the Department of Housing Preservation and Development (DHPD), but they have not been included in the research, because in the Dutch and the English case most of these activities are carried out by housing associations. This would make the comparison out of balance, since the NYCHA, for instance, employs around 15,000 people.

## References

Neuman, M. (2003a) Do plans and zoning matter?, *Planning*, Vol. (December): 28–31.

# Index